LANDSCAPES OF THE JIHAD

Crises in World Politics

TARAK BARKAWI
JAMES MAYALL
BRENDAN SIMMS
editors

GÉRARD PRUNIER
Darfur—the Ambiguous Genocide

FAISAL DEVJI
Landscapes of the Jihad

MARK ETHERINGTON
Revolt on the Tigris

AHMED HASHIM
Insurgency and Counter-Insurgency in Iraq

FAISAL DEVJI

Landscapes of the Jihad

Militancy · Morality · Modernity

Cornell University Press
Ithaca, New York

Originally published in the United Kingdom by
C. Hurst & Co. (Publishers) Ltd, London.

First published 2005 by Cornell University Press

ISBN-13: 978-0-8014-4437-1 (cloth: alk. paper)
ISBN-10: 0-8014-4437-3 (cloth: alk. paper)

Printed in the United States of America

Librarians: Library of Congress Cataloging-in-Publication Data are available.

Cornell University Press strives to use environmentally responsible suppliers and materials to the fullest extent possible in the publishing of its books. Such materials include vegetable-based, low-VOC inks and acid-free papers that are recycled, totally chlorine-free, or partly composed of nonwood fibers. For further information, visit our website at www.cornellpress.cornell.edu.

Cloth printing   10 9 8 7 6 5 4 3 2

CONTENTS

ACKNOWLEDGEMENTS

I owe many debts of gratitude to those who helped me in writing this book. My interest in the ethics and politics of modern Islam was first stimulated and directed by Fazlur Rahman, my teacher at the University of Chicago. Among those who read earlier drafts of various chapters and responded with guidance and suggestions are Arjun Appadurai, Carol Breckenridge, Leslie Dunton-Downer, Javed Gaya, Thomas Blom Hansen, Ronald Inden, Sanjay Iyer, Naveeda Khan, Uday Mehta, Satya Pemmaraju, Omar Qureshi, Vyjayanthi Rao, Arshia Sattar and Neguin Yavari. Even before deciding to write on this subject, I had discussed many of its themes with Rizwan Ahmad. I owe thanks also to my editor at Hurst, Michael Dwyer, for his advice and encouragement, to Rachel Dwyer for keeping such a fine menagerie, and to the anonymous reviewers of my manuscript. In Mumbai Christophe Carvalho's generous hospitality was matched only by his skill in finding a quiet place where I could write.

I am grateful also for the support of the Yale Center for International and Area Studies and especially to its Committee on South Asian Studies.

New Haven, March 2005   FAISAL DEVJI

PREFACE

I was in Dar-es-Salaam, the town of my birth, on August 7, 1998, when the American embassy was blown up in a car bomb attack, almost simultaneously with the one in Nairobi, by Al-Qaeda operatives. As a child I had often passed the building on my way to the watery pleasures of Oyster Bay. The embassy in Dar-es-Salaam was situated in a residential suburb, so the explosion there resulted in far fewer casualties than the suicide bombing in Nairobi's city centre. Both attacks, however, were the first of their kind for Tanzania and Kenya, neither of which had experienced terrorism in their history as independent states. While both nations have significant Muslim minorities and long-standing commercial and cultural relations with ports on the Persian Gulf and Arabian Sea, neither harbours any radical or militant Islamic movement. For example the Islamic Party of Kenya, whose troubled relations with the government differ little from those of other opposition parties, calls only for democracy, development and, at most, regional autonomy. Similar is the role of the Muslim opposition along neighbouring Tanzania's Indian Ocean coast.

Although Tanzania and Kenya had no history of Islamic radicalism, Al-Qaeda had insinuated itself into the urban life of Nairobi and Dar-es-Salaam by exploiting the long-standing cultural and commercial relations between East Africa, South Asia and the Middle East—which allowed it to recruit the local Muslims without whom no attack would have been possible. These links had never been completely innocuous, serving in the past to traffic slaves as well as ivory and spices, and more recently to smuggle goods of all kinds, including gemstones from African mines to Indian markets, and heroin en route from Afghanistan and Pakistan to Europe and the Americas. But such transactions are by no means a Muslim monopoly: Hindu merchants trade in acetic anhydride, which is used to convert low-grade opium into heroin, Roman Catholic *mafiosi* launder money in casinos and resorts frequented by Italian tourists, while South African Protestants are acquiring industrial enterprises and grabbing market share. The routes of crime and commerce that traverse East Africa were already globalized by the time Al-Qaeda arrived.

The two attacks also integrated this peripheral region into globalization by including it within a new, American-dominated, security regime, whereby Tanzania and Kenya suddenly found themselves part of the military and financial networks of global power. Israel's offer to assist them with not only relief aid but also security cooperation signalled their formal absorption as bit players in the politics of the Middle East. Kenya in particular had been the political and economic centre of equatorial Africa since colonial times, with Nairobi serving as the regional headquarters for international banks and multinational corporations. This role was no doubt helped by the fact that Kenya has always remained a politically stable, if not entirely democratic, bastion of pro-Western capitalism, its geographical location helping to make it an international commercial hub. Kenya's position on the Indian Ocean links it to South and West Asia, while affording it a coastline with sheltered naval berths, but its troubled border with Somalia to the north also places it close to a flashpoint of war and terror.

If the port of Mombasa is home to a shifting population of Somali refugees and an entrepot for smuggled goods transported across the Horn of Africa from the Red Sea, Nairobi is the base from which diplomacy and espionage in the region is co-ordinated. Following the bombing of the American embassy there, Osama bin Laden claimed that it had been the largest US listening post in equatorial Africa, and therefore a major player in the war in Somalia, from which the United States had been forced to withdraw so ignominiously in 1993. Indeed for Al-Qaeda Somalia is significant not only as a base, but also because it represents the possibility of America's military humiliation in the Muslim world, and as such it is an example that Bin Laden has repeatedly invoked. By bringing together all these factors and, as it were crystallizing them in a single event, the twin attacks on Nairobi and Dar-es-Salaam catapulted Tanzania and Kenya into globalization's big league. After all, it was in East Africa that Al-Qaeda first emerged as a global network, and so it was here, too, that America's global war on terror began.

Apart from becoming a global phenomenon in its own right, Al-Qaeda also served as an agent of globalization in East Africa. Its bombing of American embassies there integrated the region within the global networks of militant Islam as much as it integrated it within a global security regime administered by the United States. In fact it is difficult to tell where one form of integration ends and the other begins, so closely are they connected in the processes of globalization. It was precisely this blurring of lines that explains the anger ordinary Kenyans and Tanzanians manifested towards the United States in the aftermath of the attacks—an anger as deep as that directed towards Al-Qaeda. Why did the Americans have to bring conflict wherever they went? Why did they build their embassies in the middle of crowded cities knowing as they did of the security risks involved? Why did they appear to be more concerned with the wellbeing of their own personnel than with the hundreds of Africans killed and injured during the attacks? This anger had little if anything to do with anti-American feeling and was as common among Christians as it was among Muslims. Was it perhaps their unequal integration into global networks of terror and security that the residents of Nairobi and Dar-es-Salaam recognized in these complaints—for which the distinction between Al-Qaeda and the United States was irrelevant?

The symbolic form of this integration became evident immediately after the attacks. For one thing these events were initially made available to us in the region in the same way as they were to those outside it, by way of international news outlets like CNN or the BBC. I remember being part of large groups in public places watching reports emanating from Atlanta or London that dealt with what was happening just a few miles from where we stood. To some extent this was simply the expansion into the public sphere of well-established private habits of listening to the BBC World Service to find out what our state-controlled media was keeping from us. However once local media, too, started broadcasting excerpts from these international services, it became clear that what we were witnessing in Dar-es-Salaam was our own elevation to the level of global spectacle. Thanks to Al-Qaeda as much as to the United States, we had finally achieved global recognition. The echoes of this recognition have not yet died down, for the name Dar-es-Salaam, which had for so many years meant practically nothing over large parts of the globe, now possesses a sinister familiarity, which I am reminded of whenever I present my passport to an immigration officer.

Great differences of aim and organization separate Al-Qaeda and the United States. But there is a sense in which they come together

as agents of globalization. The attacks on Nairobi and Dar-es-
Salaam, the political and commercial centres of two poor countries
that are of no consequence in the comity of nations, nevertheless
signalled the emergence of two kinds of global network—one of
terror and the other of security, to employ the US administration's
terminology. What this means for East Africans differs from what it
means for Americans, to say nothing of what it might mean for the
advocates of militant Islam wherever they live. Kenyans and Tanzanians of all religious persuasions, who were not so long ago the
victims of Al-Qaeda, today wear T-shirts bearing the image of
Osama bin Laden. Is this for Islamic, anti-Western or Third Worldist
reasons? All three explanations are true to some extent and yet
none of them is, for the jihad makes Islam into an agent as well as a
product of globalization by liberating it from its specific content.
Islam becomes a global 'fact' by destroying its own traditions and
recycling their fragments in novel ways. This destruction affects
not only Muslims caught up in holy war, but also those non-
Muslims who must comprehend Islam as a global fact. T-shirts
bearing Bin Laden's portrait, then, neither represent nor indeed
stereotype Islam as a known entity. They rather empty its name of
all traditional content and use it in in the most diverse of ways.

By the time the attacks of 1998 gave way to those of 2001, this
time on American soil, Islam had become a global phenomenon—
not simply as the faith of millions, but as a word that, very much like
"America", was now part of everyone's vocabulary, demanding
from everyone an opinion about itself. With its cataclysmic arrival
in New York and Washington on the eleventh of September, Al-
Qaeda's jihad ceased to be a foreign or alien subject to become the
very stuff of American popular and political culture, finally making
a home for Islam in the West. All those who had campaigned to have

Islam better known and adequately represented in America were suddenly granted their wish thanks to these attacks, which were responsible for disseminating a new image of a good, kind and gentle Islam that was opposed to Al-Qaeda's jihad as its malign perversion. This image of Muslim virtue was broadcast from the very steps of the White House and through every conceivable medium of communication, so that it was only the threat of Islam that made possible its recognition as a religion of peace. This is the least of the jihad's ironies, though one remarked on by no less a person than Osama bin Laden himself.

On my first visit to the United States following the attacks of September 2001 I heard the various theological meanings of jihad being discussed on a local radio station, with any number of Arabic words uttered un-translated. The programme's listeners were informed that the term jihad had the general meaning of effort rather than the particular one of holy war, and that there existed in medieval Muslim thought a distinction between the greater or spiritual jihad against one's own evil impulses and the lesser or military one against an infidel enemy. It struck me then that the American presenters and audiences of this show were probably better informed about certain aspects of Islam than were most Muslims, a fact borne out by the dramatic rise in sales of the Quran and other books about Islam that also followed the attacks. When the Quran is on the *New York Times* best-seller list, are we not justified in saying that Islam has become an American phenomenon, to the degree that Americans might even be more interested in and informed about it than are Muslims? This is demonstrated by the fact that Islam no longer remains the preserve of academic or religious specialists but has become a subject upon which anybody can pronounce—because it has indeed become part not just of American but also of global culture.

The specialists who had once interpreted Islam for the public may not be entirely happy with this turn of events. As a staple of popular culture the jihad fought by Al-Qaeda has destroyed their specialized role of interpretation by eliminating the distance between America and the Muslim world that had made this role possible in the first place. Through the pervasiveness of its violence and the ubiquity of its visual impact, Al-Qaeda's jihad allows such specialists less and less room for mediation, even going so far as to fulfil their task of representing Islam by itself. Worse, the globalization of Muslim militancy makes old-fashioned forms of scholarly and religious expertise redundant, for its advocates can no longer be defined by their adherence to some peculiar tradition or place of origin because they are themselves mobile citizens of a global society. Very few Al-Qaeda operatives, for instance, have a religious education, most having been trained within secular institutions and in technical fields, and many are as familiar with the infidel West as with any other place. These men are already inside the world of their enemies and can no longer be described as an outside threat in any sense.

The bombings in Nairobi and Dar-es-Salaam, or in New York and Washington, represent the emergence of distinct cultures of terror and security in the form of global networks. Rather than seeing Tanzania, Kenya or the United States only as contexts for Al-Qaeda's jihad their bombings in fact produced it as a global entity. This new world produced by the jihad as the site of its own globalization can be described as a landscape. I use the word landscape here to describe the patterns of belief and practice that are produced by the actions of Al-Qaeda, irrespective of its members' intentions. For it is only in this way that such a network becomes global, rather than via theories or doctrines that are passed down to its members only to be realized in action. The attacks of 1998 and 2001 made Al-Qaeda a global phenomenon not simply because they projected the group into becoming a household name, but because they transformed the old worlds of terrorism and security into a variety of new global landscapes. This book does not aim to provide a sociology of Al-Qaeda's jihad but rather the reverse: to encourage us to reflect on its landscapes of global effect by a process of abstraction that is signalled by my profligate use of "the jihad" as a term to describe the global nature of Al-Qaeda's militancy in a conceptual way. The question I wish to address is also a broadly conceptual one: how does Islam become a global phenomenon in Al-Qaeda's jihad?

Studies of Al-Qaeda's jihad tend to focus on its violence, thus bringing together the most divergent intellectual and political opinions into a single narrative seeking to explain the causes and contexts of this violence. Eminent scholars of Islam such as Bernard Lewis link Al-Qaeda's violence to the nature of Islam itself, tracing its ancestry to the beginnings of Muslim history. John Esposito, another renowned authority on Islam, disagrees with this ancestral argument and links the violence of Al-Qaeda's jihad to political and economic causes of more recent vintage. At stake in this disagreement are not only rival conceptions of history, one emphasizing the role of continuity and the other of change, but also rival political positions. Lewis, then, is accused of being anti-Muslim by making violence central to Islam, while Esposito is accused of being an apologist for Muslim violence by denying its centrality. Both men, however, agree that violence is the most important thing about Al-Qaeda's jihad, and devote their energies to explaining its causes and contexts. Given the scale of such violence, this attention is understandable, but it is not therefore justified. For Al-Qaeda's violence, while certainly the most visible aspect of its jihad, is also linked to a whole world of beliefs and practices that remains invisible in much scholarly writing on the subject. This invisible world of ethical, sexual, aesthetic and other forms of behaviour is far more extensive than the jihad's realm of violence. By setting Al-Qaeda's violence within this world of beliefs and practices, then, I hope to gauge its power and durability and move beyond the narrow concerns of strategy and security.

Jihad has not always played a prominent role in the Muslim past and will not do so in its future. However egregious Al-Qaeda's militancy, it is like that of any other movement—bound for containment, compromise or defeat. Such violence is not even the most important thing about its jihad: Al-Qaeda's importance in the long run lies not in its pioneering a new form of networked militancy, which is interesting enough in its own right, but instead in its fragmentation of traditional structures of Muslim authority within new global landscapes. This might seem an anodyne statement to make, though not when one considers that Al-Qaeda's jihad may already have done more than any previous movement, secular or religious, liberal or conservative, to throw open the world of Islam to new ways of conceiving the future. It does this not only by breaking down the old-fashioned narratives of clerical, mystical and even fundamentalist authority, along with their respective forms of organization, but also by recombining these dispersed elements in extraordinarily novel ways. By "landscapes of the jihad", then, I refer to the new patterns of belief and practice, so pregnant with future possibilities, that have emerged as the global consequences of Al-Qaeda's actions.

1

EFFECTS WITHOUT CAUSES

Towards the end of *The 9/11 Commission Report* its authors make the following remarks about the globalization of Al-Qaeda's jihad:

The 9/11 attack was an event of surprising disproportion. [...] It was carried out by a tiny group of people, not enough to man a full platoon. Measured on a governmental scale, the resources behind it were trivial. The group itself was dispatched by an organization based in one of the poorest, most remote, and least industrialized countries on earth. [...] To us, Afghanistan seemed very far away. To members of al Qaeda, America seemed very close. In a sense, they were more globalized than we were.[1]

It was indeed the "surprising disproportion" between Al-Qaeda's severely limited means and seemingly limitless ends that made a global movement of its jihad. And therefore it was the very distance between a poor country like Afghanistan and a rich one like America that made its members "more globalized than we were". Such a thesis is not paradoxical, since all it does is recognize that the local causes of Al-Qaeda's jihad—men, money, motives and munitions alike—have vanished into the immensity of their own global effects. This jihad is global not because it controls people, places and circumstances over vast distances, for Al-Qaeda's control of such things is negligible, as *The 9/11 Report* testifies, but for precisely the opposite reason: because it is too weak to participate in such a politics of control. For an instrumental politics of this sort to be possible, after all, some proportion between its causes and effects is required, whereas the global consequences of Al-Qaeda's jihad have outstripped its local causes, and so have exceeded its intentions, to take on a life of their own well beyond the politics of control.

Politics had dealt with moments of excess in the past, when the unintended consequences of its actions spun out of control, but these moments did not displace political intentionality as such. So while there is nothing new in the story of consequences that outstrip their causes, creating a landscape of their own beyond any politics of control, Al-Qaeda's jihad has become globalized only within such a landscape of unintended and even accidental effects. Terrorist movements of the past, whose equally dispersed acts of violence were intended to keep their causes at the centre of international concern, had also stretched the link between these causes and their effects to breaking-point. A telling example of this is found in Jean Genet's memoir of the Palestinian movement in the 1970s, which before the *intifada* was dominated by expatriate groups. Its politics, too, was expatriated in acts of international terrorism, for whose effects the often unseen and inaccessible Palestinian homeland functioned as an almost mythical cause. At least this is how Genet describes the fantasies of Palestinian militants whom he knew:

"Our Palestinian graves have fallen from planes all over the world, with no cemeteries to mark them. Our dead have fallen from one point in the Arab nation to form an imaginary continent. And if Palestine never came down from the Empire of Heaven to dwell upon earth, would we be any less real?"

So sang one of the fedayeen, in Arabic.

"The lash of outrage was urgent. Yet here we are, a divine people, on the brink of exhaustion, sometimes close to catastrophe, and with about as much political power as Monaco," answered another.

"We are the sons of peasants. Placing our cemeteries in heaven; boasting of our mobility; building an abstract empire with one pole in Bangkok and the other in Lisbon and its capital here, with somewhere a garden of artificial flowers lent by Bahrain or Kuwait; terrorizing the whole world; making airports put up triumphal arches for us, tinkling like shop doorbells—all this to do in reality what smokers of joints only dream of. But has there ever been a dynasty that didn't build its thousand-year reign on a sham?"

So sang a third fedayeen.[2]

The disproportion between a Palestinian cause "with about as much political power as Monaco", and the international terror that was its effect, certainly bears comparison to Al-Qaeda's jihad. Also comparable was the national cause of Palestine being rendered mythical within its own international effects. Yet these Palestinian excesses were finally legitimized within an order of intentionality dedicated to the establishment of a national state. What makes today's jihad different is the increasing ordinariness of such excesses, whose global effects exist outside the politics of control, and which are detached from its traditional categories, like that of statehood. As the kind of acts that have moved beyond the rationality of intentions, such excesses now characterise the totality of the jihad's action, which has lost intentionality because it has lost control over its own global environment. For instance the attacks of 9/11, immaculately planned and executed though they were, lacked intentionality because Al-Qaeda could neither control nor even predict their global repercussions. Hence the actions of this jihad, while they are indeed meant to accomplish certain ends, have become more ethical than political in nature, since they have resigned control over their own effects, thus becoming gestures of duty or risk rather

than acts of instrumentality properly speaking.[3] This might be why
a network such as Al-Qaeda, unlike terrorist or fundamentalist
groups of the past, has no coherent vision or plan for the future.

It is perhaps their lack of political control, and therefore also of
intentionality, that explains why groups engaged in the jihad, unlike
"classical" terrorist outfits, appear to find it so difficult to claim
responsibility for their acts. It is one thing to name and laud martyrs
who have given their lives for the struggle, but another to take
credit for their actions. Osama bin Laden, for example, is generally
suspected simply of denying his role in such actions, or of false
modesty, when he insists on limiting his responsibility for the
various attacks of which he has been accused merely to instigation
or incitement.[4] But when we consider that Bin Laden also, and no
matter how disingenuously, sees these acts merely as the reflections
of oppressive conditions in the Muslim world, it becomes clear that
for him such actions are themselves only effects that have moved
well beyond the politics of causes, intentions, mobilization and the
like.[5] Indeed Olivier Roy, in his book *Globalised Islam*, argues that Al-
Qaeda's jihad does not in fact result from oppressive or disturbed
conditions in the Muslim world, and especially not in the Middle
East, because its fighters often have no experience of such conditions, and in any case tend not to involve themselves in the political struggles of their own countries, choosing instead to battle in
more exotic locations like Bosnia, Chechnya and Afghanistan.
According to Roy, then, the global jihad has to be distinguished
from local struggles not simply by its geographical sweep, but also
because it has become an individual duty for which these causes
have been reduced to abstractions. He even suggests that such local
struggles exist for it only as stereotypes, their anti-imperialist content being taken over wholesale from the international Left.[6]

Al-Qaeda's refusal to take responsibility for acts like those of 9/ 11 (or to do so only very ambiguously) is worth reflecting upon, because it distinguishes the jihad from terrorism as we have known it since the nineteenth century, for which the recognition achieved by such claims to responsibility was crucial. Given the attenuation of intentional action in a global environment, where its effects can no longer be predicted or controlled, this anonymity or ambiguity of responsibility in the jihad becomes an illustration of the anonymity or ambiguity of intentionality itself within a global dispensation. In this respect Osama bin Laden's speculations on the causes of 9/11, as reported in an interview with the Pakistani newspaper *Ummat* on September 28, 2001, are telling indeed:

The United States should try to trace the perpetrators of these attacks within itself; the people who are a part of the US system, but are dissenting against it. Or those who are working for some other system; persons who want to make the present century as a century of conflict between Islam and Christianity so that their own civilization, nation, country, or ideology could survive. They can be anyone, from Russia to Israel and from India to Serbia. In the US itself, there are dozens of well-organized and well-equipped groups, which are capable of causing a large-scale destruction. Then you cannot forget the American-Jews, who are annoyed with President Bush ever since the elections in Florida and want to avenge [*sic*] him.

Then there are intelligence agencies in the US, which require billions of dollars worth of funds from the Congress and the government every year. This [funding issue] was not a big problem till [*sic*] the existence of the former Soviet Union but after that the budget of these agencies has been in danger. They needed an enemy. So, they first started propaganda against Usama and Taleban and then this incident happened. You see, the Bush Administration approved a budget of 40 billion dollars. Where will this huge amount go? It will be provided to the same agencies, which need huge funds and want to exert their importance. Now they will spend the money for their expansion and for increasing their importance. I will give you an example. Drug smugglers from all over the world are in contact with the US secret agencies. These agencies do not want to eradicate narcotics cultivation and trafficking because their importance will be diminished. The people in the US Drug Enforcement Department are encouraging drug trade so that they could show performance and get millions of dollars worth of budget. General Noriega was made a drug baron by the CIA and, in need, he was made a scapegoat. In the same way, whether it is President Bush or any other US President, they cannot bring Israel to justice for its human rights abuses or to hold it accountable for such crimes. What is this? Is it not that there exists a government within the government in the United States? That secret government must be asked as to who carried out the attacks.[7]

What Osama bin Laden says in this lengthy statement is far more interesting than why he says it—presumably to evade retribution for the attacks of 9/11. For one thing the variety of possible causes he invokes for these attacks are ones of *realpolitik* alone and have no religious dimension, being very unlike his statements on the jihad in this respect. And for another they consist of conspiracy theories and half-truths that have an all-too familiar ring, possessing therefore a plural audience rather than a singularly Muslim one. Indeed some of these possible causes, like the secret "government within the government", have a distinctly American provenance and are well established in that country's popular culture. All Osama bin Laden need have done was to watch a television show like the X-Files or a film by Oliver Stone to concoct the statements that he uttered in his interview. Such causes are nothing but stereotypes, and are I think deployed as such, because responsibility has itself become a kind of stereotype in a landscape of global effects—where acts lose intentionality because they can no longer control their own outcomes.

Osama bin Laden is indiscriminate in his invocation of domestic and foreign causes for the attacks of 9/11, thus erasing any distinction between the two and operating instead at a purely global level, one in which the sheer range of the contradictory possibilities on offer demolishes intentionality itself as an explanatory category. After all, even if a single group was responsible for the attacks on America, the very existence of so many alternative culprits dissipates this responsibility in political terms—for they could have been perpetrated by someone else, and therefore might have produced very different consequences. Since none of these possibilities is foreclosed in Osama bin Laden's interview, they continue to remain live issues, each with a similar potential for destruction that stems from the very nature of American power, rather than from the responsibility of any autonomous actor. This is made explicit in Bin Laden's description of the domestic American politics that he suggests made US agencies dealing with narcotics or crime complicit in attacks such as those of 9/11. With this argument political intentionality becomes impossible because it possesses little if any autonomy, since Bin Laden is unable to separate the domestic causes of 9/11 from the foreign ones, or the local from the global, resulting in the disintegration of causality itself amid universal complicity. We shall see below that the only kind of action for which the jihad claims full responsibility is that paradoxical and individualistic act of self-destruction called martyrdom. Is martyrdom, then, the only way of rescuing moral autonomy because it is the only act for which responsibility can be claimed in the jihad?

New markets for our traders

There follow two examples of what I mean by the landscape of accidental effects within which a network like Al-Qaeda becomes global beyond a politics of intentionality. First are the East African attacks with which both Al-Qaeda and the new security regime administered by the United States began their global histories. The bombing in 1998 of US embassies in Kenya and Tanzania, followed by retaliatory missile strikes against military bases run by a Saudi expatriate in Afghanistan, as well as a pharmaceutical plant in Sudan, together comprise a remarkably dispersed sequence of events in which the various killers and victims, causes and effects, countries and targets involved, shared neither history nor geography and had nothing to do with each other. They came to be related by accident rather than design. Yet it was only in this temporary configuration of disparate peoples and places that Al-Qaeda's jihad was established as a global movement.

Although the countries attacked and most of those killed in Eastern Africa and Central Asia were unrelated to one another in every sense, not one even being denounced as another's enemy, we cannot dismiss them simply as extras: the civilian casualties, innocent victims or collateral damage caught up in Al-Qaeda's attacks and America's retaliation. After all it was the variety of peoples and countries involved, more than anything else, which transformed these events into a series of global effects. Indeed it is the very distance of the jihad's effects from its proclaimed causes that makes it into the global movement it is. What connected Kenyans, Tanzanians, Sudanese, Americans and Afghans within this order of global effects, then, was mere contingency, for they were related only formally and even despite themselves, beyond any schema of Al-Qaeda's intentions.

The choice of Nairobi and Dar-es-Salaam as targets, therefore, had nothing to do with their political or military status, nor even with the presence of American embassies there, since this is a commonplace of capital cities the world over. It depended instead on the most local of causes, willing agents in the region, who transformed it into something quite random, since without such agents any other city may—or may not—have been targeted in as random a manner. Unlike its causes, then, which might be tied to shared objectives such as the removal of oppressive regimes in the Islamic world, a common interest in establishing a virtuous Islamic order, or ideas in common about the anti-Muslim policies of the United States and its allies, the jihad's effects agglomerate diverse countries and peoples into relations that are divorced from any prior history and display little if any commonality. Yet it is precisely in this accidental universe that the jihad is globalized as a series of effects that have lost sight of their own causes.

A second example of a landscape of accidents within which the jihad becomes global are the commercial metaphors that recur in descriptions of Al-Qaeda's operations. Like companies in the world economy, to which they are often compared, participants in the global jihad have neither the ability nor the inclination to control the territories within which they operate in any old-fashioned sense. Their relationship with these territories can instead be seen as a series of indirect and speculative investments. Just as with players in the global economy, participants in the jihad are drawn by their investments into a world that does not operate according to their intentions but seems to possess a life of its own. While the attacks of 9/11, for instance, were meticulously planned, they were at the same time completely speculative as far as their effects were concerned, since these could neither be predicted with any degree of certainty, nor controlled in any fashion. Practices of terror in the jihad, then, are akin to those of risk in the global economy. That companies and markets do not serve only as metaphors for the jihad is evident in Al-Qaeda's operation of commercial enterprises in the Sudan and elsewhere. Moreover the group's internal communications are peppered with references to markets and financial speculation, to the extent of Al-Qaeda being itself referred to as "the company". Here, for instance, is a coded letter dated May 3, 2001, found in Afghanistan after the fall of the Taliban in the computer of Ayman al-Zawahiri, Osama bin Laden's Egyptian lieutenant and founder of the Al-Jihad group. It is followed by a decoded translation:

We have been trying to go back to our main, previous activity. The most important step was the opening of the school. We have made it possible for the teachers to find openings for profitable trade. As you know, the situation down in the village has become bad for the traders. Our relatives in the south have abandoned the market, and we are suffering from international monopoly companies. But Allah enlightened us with His mercy when the Omar Brothers Company was established. It has opened new markets for our traders and provided them with an opportunity to re-arrange their accounts. One benefit of trading here is the congregation in one place of all the traders who came over from everywhere and began working for this company. Acquaintance and cooperation have grown, especially between us and Abdullah Contractors Company.[8]

We have been trying to go back to our military activities. The most important step was the declaration of unity with al-Qaeda. We have made it possible for the mujahideen to find an opening for martyrdom. As you know, the situation down in Egypt has become bad for the mujahideen: our members in Upper Egypt have abandoned military action, and we are suffering from international harassment. [...] But Allah enlightened us with His mercy when the Taliban came to power. It has opened doors of military action for our mujahideen and provided them with an opportunity to re-arrange their forces. One benefit of performing jihad here is the congregation in one place of all the mujahideen who came from everywhere and began working for the Islamic Jihad Organisation. Acquaintance and cooperation have grown, especially between us and al-Qaeda.[9]

Commercial analogies are employed to describe the failure and consequent abandonment of local struggles in Egypt, not accidentally called the "village", for a global mission. And for such a mission, operating in a shifting landscape of speculative invest-ments, political relations are no longer tied to common histories or geographies, but are the result of strategies and alliances grounded by global market forces. These are not the kinds of relations that had characterized national struggles in the past, which brought together people who shared a history and a geography into a polit-ical arena defined by processes of intentionality and control. Unlike the politics of national movements, the jihad is grounded not in the propagation of ideas or similarity of interests and conditions, so much as in the contingent relations of a global marketplace. Such relations, more than any traditional mobilization of people for or against a particular objective, make this jihad into the global phe-nomenon that it is. This might explain why there appears to have been so much disagreement within Al-Qaeda itself, as well as among its Arab fighters and their non-Arab partners in Afghanistan, for we shall see later that an old-fashioned politics of collective unity has little or no place in its jihad.[10]

What does this mean for an old-fashioned politics of intention-ality, built upon the mobilization of people over historical needs, ideas or interests? How is politics thought about differently in a landscape of effects whose inhabitants are related by accident rather than by intent? Such questions cannot be confined to the jihad, and are characteristic of global movements more generally, which are also unable either to predict or control the effects of their own actions on a global scale. These are movements whose practices are ethical rather than political in nature because they have been trans-formed into gestures of risk and duty rather than acts of instrumen-tality. However instrumental their intentions, the politics of such movements are invariably transformed into ethics at a global level—think, for instance, of environmentalism, the anti-global-ization protests, the supporters of disarmament, anti-abortion groups and the like. In this sense the jihad stands alongside these movements, whose spectacular demonstrations of strength escape a politics of intentionality and control that is organized around some common history of needs, interests or ideas, to create a landscape of relations in which very little, if anything, is shared. So the worldwide mass demonstrations of 2003 protesting the impending war in Iraq were not only the largest global demonstrations yet seen, they also brought together individuals and groups who possessed neither organizational nor ideological commonality of any sort. Like such movements, Greenpeace, for instance, the global effects of the jihad bring together allies and enemies of the most heterogeneous character, who neither know nor communicate each with the other, and who in addition share almost nothing by way of a prior history.[11]

Because of its predominance among global movements, resulting from the enormity of the forces it unleashes, the jihad might provide responses to the questions I have posed above that will come in future to define the behaviour of its peers. Violence, though definitive of the jihad today, is probably the least important of these responses, and likely the most short-lived compared to the other transformations that Al-Qaeda has wrought. Indeed such violence might well represent the final agony of an old-fashioned politics centred in a specific geography and based on a history of common needs, interests or ideas. Rather than marking the emergence of a new kind of Muslim politics, in other words, Al-Qaeda's jihad may signal the end of such politics. Far more important than violence might be the emergence of a new kind of global practice in the accidental and unintended effects of the jihad, such as wider demands for democratisationi in the Middle East, Pakistan and Indonesia. Like other global movements, but perhaps more clearly than them, the jihad displaces politics by ethics as a way of engaging with its accidental universe. It is in this sense only the most radical example of the proliferating debates on ethics that increasingly mark global entities like non-governmental organizations and multi-national corporations.

A whirlpool of contradictions

A videotape was recorded sometime in November 2001 and re-leased by Al-Qaeda to the press in December. It showed, among other things, Osama bin Laden's reactions to the 9/11 attacks. His response was delivered not directly to camera but as part of a con-versation with some Saudi visitors to Afghanistan:

Those youths who conducted the operations did not accept any fiqh [school of Islamic law] in the popular terms, but they accepted the fiqh that the Prophet Muhammad brought. Those young men… said in deeds, in New York and Washington, speeches that overshadowed all other speeches made everywhere in the world. The speeches are understood by both Arabs and non-Arabs—even by the Chinese. It is above all (what) the media said. Some of them said in Holland, at one of the centers, the number of people who accepted Islam during the days that followed the operations were more than the people who accepted Islam in the last eleven years. I heard someone on Islamic radio who owns a school in America say: "We don't have time to keep up with the demands of those who are asking about Islamic books to learn about Islam." This event made people think. […] which benefited Islam greatly.[12]

What is of interest here is not why Bin Laden uttered these sen-tences, their truth or untruth, nor even what they might reveal about the workings of his mind, but rather what they tell us about the jihad as a series of global effects. For one thing Bin Laden made no distinction between the attacks themselves and their coverage by the media, to the degree that the destruction wrought is upstaged in his comments by the global impact of their diffusion. What was noteworthy about this media attention was not the fear or terror that it inspired, but rather the proselytization to Islam that it supposedly facilitated. Bin Laden's comments on the missionary role of the jihad are by no means uncommon but have been repeated any number of times in his statements and interviews, seeming, indeed, to provide the larger purpose for its actions, even if this is unintended and only accidental.[13]

On the one hand, then, Bin Laden's reflections upon the attacks in America supersede and even disregard the obvious politics of intentionality in which they were mired, organized around histories of common needs, interests or ideas that include familiar issues like American support for the Israeli occupation of Palestine or its quest to control Middle Eastern oil supplies through pliant local regimes. Even the intentions of the media, whose alleged misrepresentation of Muslims is otherwise much criticized, are here passed by so that Bin Laden can concentrate on their accidental global effects, in this case the preaching of Islam. On the other hand these comments by the founder of Al-Qaeda make the claim that the globalization of the jihad lies precisely in the unintended consequences of its acts. This claim is an important one, and worth examining.

Osama bin Laden describes the events of September the eleventh not as hostile or vengeful actions so much as a set of communications. Indeed he calls the acts of the hijackers speeches that were understood by everyone, Arab and non-Arab, even by the Chinese. And how were these speeches so widely understood? Because they were disconnected from the causes and intentions not only of the attacks upon America but also of the mass media that transmitted them, instead achieving meaning as a series of global effects. It is possible to dismiss this as guesswork and to contend that all Bin Laden's statement implies is that actions speak louder than words, something he demonstrates by pointing to the sudden jump in interest about, and maybe also conversion to, Islam following the attacks. But this would be to interpret his words merely as a rhetorical flourish.

As it turns out, however, Osama bin Laden's claims about the missionary work inadvertently performed by the hijackers' actions cannot be confined to rhetoric because they possess a certain analytical weight—not least because it is exactly in this way, rather than by any traditional process of recruitment and indoctrination, that Al-Qaeda attracted its own myrmidons. So Bin Laden's assertion that more people in Holland were brought to Islam by the attacks of September 11 than by traditional forms of preaching there over the past eleven years, suggests his criticism of such local practices of proselytization as well as his recognition of the jihad's global novelty. After all the fact that his name, cause and even lexicon were adopted by radical Muslim groups around the world following Al-Qaeda's actions in America could not fail to impress any observer. Nor could the allied fact fail to impress, that this wholesale if by no means undifferentiated adoption, often swamping long-standing political terminologies, was undertaken by people who had perhaps never before heard either of Osama bin Laden or Al-Qaeda. And all this was frequently accomplished with no direct contact between any of these groups, not even in the form of circulating pamphlets or videotapes. An intriguing illustration of the jihad's globalization as a series of effects was provided by the posters brandished in support of Al-Qaeda during demonstrations in the Bangladeshi capital of Dhaka in October 2001. These consisted of images of Osama bin Laden that had been taken off internet sites, including an American one in which he was paired with the puppet character "Bert" from the children's television show *Sesame Street*.[14]

The kind of proselytization that Bin Laden discusses in his reflections on the attacks of 9/11 dispenses entirely with old-fashioned concerns about the ritual and doctrinal details of Islamic practice, as well as the importance of linguistic training and correct textual exegesis, all of which are characteristic of conversion as a local activity organized in terms of intentionality. These mainstays of Muslim preaching heretofore are not exactly dismissed by Al-Qaeda's founder, but instead put aside for other people and other places, thus making possible the transmission of Islam's message universally, among Arabs and non-Arabs, including even the Chinese. This lack of concern with the details of correct Islamic practice is in fact signalled in his opening comments, when Bin Laden speaks of the hijackers following no accepted form of Islamic law. Such a statement, while common among Sunni radicals, is of course anathema to all but the most mystical, heretical or secular of Muslim groups, in whose company the jihad thus places itself. The jihad's destruction of inherited forms of Islamic authority puts it in a paradoxically intimate relationship with other groups that it might well consider beyond the pale of Islam.

Bin Laden's remark about the hijackers of 9/11 belonging to no accepted school of Islamic law makes perfect sense in view of their diverse nationalities and backgrounds, but more importantly in terms of the apparent absence of any religious uniformity among them. So while the chief hijacker, the Egyptian citizen and German resident Muhammad Atta, was known to have been very pious, some of his companions do not seem to have been averse to consuming alcohol, gambling in Las Vegas or attending a lap-dancing club in the days before their final flight. This is a pattern that repeats itself among participants in the jihad, and especially in its martyrdom operations. The following press description of the terrorist suspects wanted in connection with the Madrid railway station bombing of April 2004 is entirely typical:

Many of them appeared westernized and integrated into the Spanish community, with a liking for football, fashion, drinking and Spanish girlfriends, say Spanish press reports. [...] Jamal Ahmidan, 33, thought to be one of the cell commanders with links to al-Qaeda, also died in the blast. [...] Little is known about Ahmidan, known as El Chino or Mowgli, except that his family owns clothes shops in the Lavapies area of Madrid. [...] Ahmidan is also said to have seemed happily integrated in Spanish society, whose Spanish friends are said to have included women who sported crop tops, tattoos and piercings.[15]

The puzzlement that lurks in such press reports is palpable: how might a clandestine group of bombers for an Islamic cause be described who apparently have nothing in common? Whose members do not seem to fit into any social or psychological category, any theory of integration or alienation, and who may to cap it all be known by the names of characters in Rudyard Kipling's *Jungle Book*? The explicit breaking of certain of the inherited practices of Islam, rather than simply disputing their theological status, is a characteristic of the global jihad and bears comparison with a heretical Shia group like the medieval Assassins of Syria and Iran, or the outlaw bands found in the fiction of William S. Burroughs. Here, for example, is a telling passage from a letter to his brother discovered in one of Al-Qaeda's Afghan camps, from a Yemeni named Khalid:

I am in a whirlpool of contradictions. You cannot trust anyone here. Imagine that I have to hide the copy of the Koran you gave me for fear it might get stolen like my watch. They train us here on how to mix with the Christians and how to emulate their life style. We have to learn how to drink alcohol and to shave off our beards.[16]

Given the pious nature of many of the fighters in these Afghan camps, one should treat with scepticism Khalid's claims of their collective training in Western decadence, a course in deception that, if true, would resemble the peculiar Shia doctrine of *taqiyya* or religious dissimulation too closely to escape comment, especially in view of the widespread Sunni objections to this practice. On the other hand, as we shall see below, this ostensibly Sunni jihad borrows very freely from Shiism, adopting its doctrine of dissimulation among other things. So immediately after the attacks of 9/11 Osama bin Laden went out of his way to deny any knowledge of, let alone any responsibility for, them, going so far as to call the killing of civilians un-Islamic—a position he had repudiated earlier and would soon reverse again by citing religious authority.[17] Moreover the combination described by Khalid of highly disciplined action with completely individualised behaviour like stealing, to say nothing of drinking, is sufficiently unusual to put the so-called Al-Qaeda camps beyond any standard model of regimentation, whether religious or political. Such camps were far removed from the stern places of discipline and dedication one often imagines, for they not only included the wives and children of fighters, but also seem to have been awash with all manner of petty bickering and even fraud, just like any other institution.[18] The soft copy of a sign found on the hard drive of a computer recovered from Al-Qaeda's office in Kabul even admonishes militants for allowing strangers to wander around the premises, reminding them that it was a place of work.[19] And there is evidence to suggest that ideological indoctrination as well as disputation, though certainly not personal devotion, was forbidden.

Thus a manual of instructions, found at one of these camps after the fall of the Taliban, includes the following rule:

It is forbidden to discuss controversial matters or criticise any Islamic group or organisation or any individuals, be they imams, thinkers, leaders or politicians.[20]

If the jihad is seen as a series of global effects, the disparate character of these bombers, hijackers and would-be martyrs should come as no surprise. Because it operates in a landscape of relations that are not determined by causes and intentions, the jihad must eschew a politics that would organize people only around common beliefs or practices. In effect this means that such beliefs and practices are given over to individual rather than collective examination, although it by no means entails either a tolerant or an uncaring attitude towards them. Since participants in the jihad are connected by the contingency of effects rather than by some common substance, therefore, they share neither a psychological profile nor require any cultic or ideological uniformity to bind them together.

There is no better illustration of these points than the organizational structure of Al-Qaeda. This is famous now for being decentralized and of emulating a player in the global marketplace—a service provider perhaps, or a franchise. Like these, Al-Qaeda does not own or control all its operatives; instead it chooses to link them by providing training, or finances, and certainly information and contacts. So the 9/11 plot was proposed to and managed for Al-Qaeda by an outsider, the Pakistani Khalid Sheikh Mohammed, who is described in *The 9/11 Commission Report* as a "terrorist entrepreneur", while its disparate hijackers were often recruited upon first contact without much attention being paid to their background or indoctrination.[21] In fact apart from the interviews, statements and actions broadcast by the international media and over the

Internet, Al-Qaeda appears to have no formal procedure of re-cruitment or indoctrination, not even by way of sleepers who sup-posedly lurk in mosques to trap the unwary martyrs of tomorrow. Its jihad is not a collective movement of the traditional kind, nor one that seduces alienated and vulnerable young men, but, like other global movements, attracts diverse volunteers for equally diverse reasons.[22] Already, then, we can see that however common or uncommon the goals of these groups and individuals, they are not related by any traditional practice of religious or political mobi-lization, and therefore by any politics of intentionality either.

The jihad achieves globalization within a landscape of purely accidental relations separated as if by a vast abyss from a politics of control linked to causes and intentions. Such globalization is not peripheral to any Muslim practice in the jihad but grounds all of it in its entirety. The jihad as a series of global effects, therefore, does not simply exist alongside other forms of Islamic devotion but actively subverts these latter. Not only are old methods of learning, per-suasion and practice made parochial and sometimes even redundant by the jihad, but a new kind of Muslim, too, is created in the process, one not defined by any notion of cultic uniformity. In the chapters that follow I will elaborate upon these assertions, but before doing so I turn to scholarly discussions on jihad, and partic-ularly how scholars of Islam describe its novelty.

Accounting for Al-Qaeda

Faced with what is new, and especially what is radically new, the scholar's conservative instinct is always to reach for some genealogy within which this novelty might be anchored and neutralized. In the case of the jihad this instinct works to place it in the genealogy of something called political Islam, where its ancestry is generally traced to Middle Eastern movements of the modern period like Salafism (an effort to follow the path of the early Muslims that includes within its ambit groups such as the Muslim Brotherhood) or Wahhabism (a militant effort to purify Islam named after the eighteenth-century thinker Muhammad ibn Abdul Wahhab, who lived in what is today Saudi Arabia, a country that claims to be founded on his principles). Indeed movements like the Salafis and Wahhabis are so central to the genealogies of political Islam that their presence is often updated or renewed by attaching their names with the prefix neo, as in neo-Wahhabi, but rarely with the prefix post.

A curious feature of such genealogies of the jihad is that they all originate in and remain focused specifically upon Sunni Islam and the Middle East, despite the fact that arguably the most successful examples of political Islam have been revolutionary Iran and the Hezbollah in Lebanon, both Shia movements, which among other things have contributed to an ostensibly Sunni jihad the language and practice of the "martyrdom operation", as its suicide attacks are known. Similarly the fact that the jihad today happens to be based for the most part outside the Middle East (in places like Chechnya, Afghanistan, Pakistan, India and the Philippines) among populations that have barely an inkling of Salafi or Wahhabi traditions, seems to have escaped the notice of scholarly genealogists. Apparently the very presence of Arab fighters or funding in such places is evidence enough that Salafi or Wahhabi Islam has been exported in sufficient measure to determine the nature of jihad there. That the reverse might be true, with Arab fighters and financiers importing the jihad from these regions to the Middle East, is not seriously considered, although it is certainly true of Al-Qaeda and the phenomenon of the so called Arab-Afghans, militants who returned after the anti-Soviet war in Afghanistan to their homes in the Middle East and founded new jihad movements there.

In general the importance of non-Arab Muslims and of non-Arab
Islam to the Middle East has been underestimated, as borne out by
the example of Iraq in early 2005: when Ayatullah Sistani was the
country's great Shiite authority, even though he is an Iranian whose
Arabic remains heavily accented by his native Farsi. Much of
Sistani's authority in Iraq, moreover, derives from his control and
disbursement of funds raised by Shia populations elsewhere, a very
significant portion of which come from India and Pakistan. Sistani's
constituency in the subcontinent, then, through his agent in Mumbai, might well hold a key to the Ayatullah's importance in Iraq. This
Shiite example apart, the presence of large non-Arab working populations in the Arabian Peninsula, as well as the dominance of non-
Arab Muslims in the formulation and dissemination of Islamic ideas
globally, especially in languages like English, renders nonsensical
any notion that the Arab Middle East is the original homeland of
radical Islam.

The Taliban provides a perfect illustration of the kind of movement that has repeatedly been described as a foreign import. It was
supposedly influenced by Deobandi practices from India, themselves funded and influenced by Saudi Wahhabism, and by Wahhabi
practices coming directly from Saudi Arabia—both imparted in
Pakistani seminaries, and both supposedly legalistic and scripturalist in the extreme. And yet the Taliban leader Mullah Omar chose in
Kandahar to drape himself in a mantle belonging to the Prophet and
declare himself the Commander of the Faithful, a title used for the
caliphs who were meant to be Muhammad's successors—he was in
fact flatteringly called a caliph by no less a person than Osama bin
Laden. In what way did this coronation conform to any Deobandi or
Wahhabi teaching? If anything the vision of Mullah Omar donning
the Prophet's mantle suggests Sufi and especially Shia themes, since

the latter believe in the apostolic succession of those members of Muhammad's family whom he famously covered with his cloak. And it is precisely such charismatic forms of authority that both the Deobandis and Wahhabis are supposed to execrate.

There is nothing more calculated to degrade the celebrated scripturalist or legalist forms of Islam associated with these groups, tied as they are to the authority of a class of scholarly commentators, than the institution of a self-proclaimed Commander of the Faithful—one who claimed, in addition, to have received divine instruction in his dreams. By acts such as these, the Taliban not only assumed an immediate superiority over their Saudi or Pakistani teachers, they also forced from the latter an acknowledgement of religious forms and practices that were barely dreamt of in the Deobandi and Wahhabi schools. Suddenly it seemed as if the direction of Islamic influence had been reversed, with teachers in the centre taking dictation from students on the periphery. And who can deny the wave of approval for all these Afghan innovations, mystical and even Shia though they might be, that swept the world of militant Sunnism? It is no accident then, that one of these militants interviewed by Jessica Stern in her book *Terror in the Name of God*, an Indonesian who had fought the jihad in Afghanistan, accused the Taliban precisely of being Sufi and of relying "on dreams and fantasies".[23]

The jihad is placed within genealogies of political Islam that are drawn up by systematic procedures of a racial, religious and regional apartheid that maintain what is essential to every genealogy: its purity. In the process any inconvenient fact—the importance of the Pakistani Mawdudi for both Shiites like Khomeini and prominent Salafi thinkers like the Egyptian Sayyid Qutb, let alone the influence of Sufism or Shiism on the jihad itself—must either be downplayed or erased outright. But the dispersed nature and global

effects of the jihad are putting an increasing strain on all genealogical forms of explanation, which are very difficult to sustain
when they cannot clearly be confined to some common geography,
language or religious and political tradition. Accordingly, scholarly
genealogies have now assumed the character almost of medieval
chronicles in order to defend their purity, linking the jihad's transmission to purely individual influences and encounters. So for
instance we are often reminded that Sayyid Qutb's brother
Muhammad left Egypt to teach at the King Abdul Aziz University in
Jeddah where he met a Jordanian-Palestinian student, Abdullah
Azzam, who later went to Pakistan from where he became the chief
ideologue in the Arab world of the Afghan jihad. The fact that
Azzam should then have met the Saudi citizen of Yemeni ancestry
Osama bin Laden in Peshawar comes as no surprise. While these
individual meetings are of course important in the biographies of
fighters as well as in the operations they undertake, more interesting, I think, is the possibility that they are quite irrelevant to the
jihad itself as a global movement.

Can the jihad and its global effects be reduced to individual biographies and the politics of the Middle East? Is a genealogical mode of
explanation at all credible in a situation where participants in the
jihad come from all manner of national and religious backgrounds?
Quite apart from the hijackers in New York or the bombers in
Madrid who betrayed no obvious signs of Muslim piety, we know
that in places like Afghanistan, too, fighters came from many different and even opposed Islamic affiliations that are generally kept
far apart by scholarly genealogists. One might find in Kandahar, for
example, members of the allegedly quietist or non-political group
of Indian derivation, the Tablighi Jamaat, as well as those belonging
to the Jamaat-e Islami, of Pakistani origin, who are committed to

the establishment of an Islamic state, not to mention members of the Muslim League, a political party supposedly devoted to Pakistani nationalism. But the plethora of groups, often very exclusive, participating in the jihad does not indicate their alliance for some common cause. It may however signal the fact that a global movement like the jihad depends upon the erosion of traditional religious and political allegiances for its very existence. After all we have seen that Al-Qaeda, like other global movements, possesses an extraordinarily diverse membership, one that is not united by way of any cultic or ideological commonality, to say nothing about that of class, ethnicity or personal background. Indeed it can only function as the network it is by disrupting and disregarding old-fashioned forms of political and religious allegiance.

Confronted with bastard phenomena that would sully the legitimacy of any family history, scholars of Islam are sometimes forced to retain such purity as they can by transferring these illicit offspring to another genealogy. The favourite method of doing so is to excommunicate certain practices from lineages in the Islamic tradition and attribute them to some vaguely defined modern or Western category of kinship. A consequence of this practice, especially marked among those who are not scholars of Islam, is to deny the jihad any originality by attributing even its most spectacular effects to a Western inheritance. As Reinhard Schulze has recently remarked, such attempts to include the jihad within a political tradition of Western radicalism often means that what remains of a non-Western Islam is carefully sequestered from world history, existing within a hermetically sealed genealogy of its own.[24] This closed world, then, requires only cultural sensitivity and a respect for difference, even and especially when it is being destroyed, as the American army's much-trumpeted rules of multicultural engagement in Iraq demonstrate. Indeed some of the humiliations to which American soldiers subjected Iraqi detainees in Abu Ghraib Prison may be symptoms of the army's recognition of "cultural difference", itself apparently a familiar phrase at the prison.[25] These included male nudity, especially in the presence of women, the simulation of sexual intercourse among men, masturbation and the wearing by men of women's underwear, sometimes on their heads.[26] Surely such practices betray as much awareness of "cultural difference" as multiculturalists would like, being merely the obverse side of the latter's respect?

My description above of scholarship on the jihad is a caricature if not a travesty: it does no justice to any writer on the subject but is meant instead to be a patchwork of common yet unconvincing themes in academic writing on the jihad. Most objectionable of all is the attempt to place the jihad within a genealogy of influences emanating from something called political Islam, itself sequestered from a history of modernity more generally, to which it can at most be related as a kind of reaction. Not everyone does this, of course, and Reinhard Schulze even sets himself the formidable task of interpreting the entirety of modern Islam in terms of what he calls universal history, while Roxanne Euben's study of Sayyid Qutb, *Enemy in the Mirror*, is probably the first work to locate Islamic fundamentalism within the precincts of political philosophy.[27] If my objective above was to broach the possibility of the jihad being defined in accidental terms as a series of global effects, I, too, wish to conclude this chapter by locating it within a general history of modern times.

Fundamentalist futures

The jihad has replaced what used to be called Islamic fundamentalism at the edge of Muslim militancy. This latter had been part and parcel of Cold War politics and was concerned with the founding through revolution of an ideological state, fashioned in many respects on the communist model that was so popular in Africa and Asia following the Second World War. As Seyyed Vali Reza Nasr has shown in his two books on one of the most important fundamentalist thinkers, the Pakistani Sayyid Abul Ala Mawdudi and his Jamaat-e Islami party, communist ideas about the party as vanguard of the revolution, the state as an explicitly ideological institution meant to produce a utopian society, and the like, were central to the movement.[28] With the end of the Cold War, however, and the coming into being of a global market for transactions of all kinds, the revolutionary politics meant to institute ideological states quickly began to break down. This sort of fundamentalism, after all, had enjoyed only one success in its many decades of struggle, with the Islamic Republic of Iran. But given Iran's own economic and political stagnation as a fundamentalist state, the Muslim world was confronted with what Olivier Roy has called the failure of political Islam, in his book of the same name.[29]

Unlike fundamentalism, the jihad is not concerned with political parties, revolutions or the founding of ideological states. For someone like Ayman al-Zawahiri, who comes from a fundamentalist background in the Muslim Brotherhood, struggles in particular countries are important for two reasons: because, like the Taliban's Afghanistan, they provide a base for jihad more generally, as well as for rousing Muslims internationally. In other words the particular sites of these struggles are themselves unimportant, their territories being subordinated to a larger and even metaphysical struggle for which they have become merely instrumental. Indeed by moving between Bosnia and Afghanistan, Chechnya and Iraq, the jihad displays its fundamental indifference to these territories rather than consolidating them into a single Muslim geography. It ends by de-territorializing Islam altogether, since it is not one country or another that is important, but instead Islam itself as a global entity. So in his book *Knights Under the Banner of the Prophet*, which was smuggled out of an Afghan cave to Peshawar and thence to the Arabic newspaper *Al-Sharq al-Awsat* in London, Zawahiri describes the importance of invoking the Palestinian struggle solely in terms of a way to gain the support of Arabs and Muslims:

The fact that must be acknowledged is that the issue of Palestine is the cause that has been firing up the feelings of the Muslim nation from Morocco to Indonesia for the past 50 years. In addition, it is a rallying point for all the Arabs, be they believers or non-believers, good or evil.[30]

This subordination of local to global struggles differs from the internationalism of revolutionary movements like communism both because it is based on the failure rather than success of local struggles, and because it implies the coming into being of a new global environment after the Cold War. The latter thus conceived is not seen by any proponent of the jihad who has voiced an opinion on the subject as an external event but as one intimately connected to the jihad itself. Osama bin Laden, Ayman al-Zawahiri and many others have repeatedly given credit for the collapse of the Soviet Union and the end of the Cold War to the holy warriors who they say defeated the Soviet army in Afghanistan. Whatever grain of truth there is in this claim, it demonstrates that the jihad is seen to have assumed a global role by participating in the Cold War. More than this, the end of the Cold War is considered to have catapulted the jihad into assuming, inadvertently, the global role of the Soviet Union as the only force willing to resist the absolute dominance of the United States. Thus Zawahiri:

In the wake of the USSR's collapse, the United States monopolized its military superiority to dictate its wishes to numerous governments and, as a result, has succeeded in imposing security agreements on many countries. In this way the power of the governments that are affiliated with the United States grew in the sphere of pursuing the mujahideen in many countries. Doubtlessly this had an impact on the fundamentalist movement. Still this has been a new challenge that the jihadist movement confronted with methods that can reduce its impact. It did this by turning the United States into a target.[31]

It is clear from the above that the Jewish-Crusade[r] alliance, led by the United States, will not allow any Muslim force to reach power in any of the Islamic countries. It will mobilize all its power to hit it and remove it from power. Toward that end, it will open a battlefront against it that includes the entire world. It will impose sanctions on whoever helps it, if it does not declare war against them altogether. Therefore, to adjust to this new reality we must prepare ourselves for a battle that is not confined to a single region, one that includes the apostate domestic enemy and the Jewish-Crusade[r] external enemy.[32]

The impossibility of local struggles means that local causes and intentions have finally disappeared into their own effects to create an accidental or inadvertent landscape for the jihad's globalization. The local causes or intentions behind Al-Qaeda's attacks on Washington and New York, for example, have disappeared beneath the rubble of the World Trade Center. The jihad these attacks were meant to propound has become globalized in its unintended and uncontrollable effects. In the jihad itself this globalization is reflected upon by way of a new kind of history, one very different from a fundamentalist history that was linked to a Marxist dialectic culminating in revolution. In effect this is a global history that depends upon the disintegration of traditional Muslim narratives and chronologies, as much as of modern theories of ideology and revolution, so that the events of Islam's past are emancipated for very different uses in the present.

In the jihad a global history of the West is matched at every point by its effects upon the Muslim world, which is seen as being co-extensive with it and forming a mirror history of the West itself. Apart from the medieval relations between Muslims, Christians and Jews, as well as the impact of European colonialism and the Cold War upon Islam, this history is composed of actions and person-alities that have very little to do with Muslim tradition but are para-sitical upon Western accounts of Islamic history. These include Saladin and the waging of the Crusades, the conquest and loss of Muslim Spain, Napoleon's invasion of Egypt and the decline of the Ottoman Empire. As is evident from the use of the term Crusaders for the United States and its allies, these historical subjects are by no means confined to the past but available for productive use today, very deliberately translating the history of the West into Islamic terms. For example the title of Zawahiri's *Knights Under the Banner of the Prophet* refers to the crusading Knights of the Holy Sepulchre.

This global history brings together Judaism, Christianity and Islam in a single landscape. And it is the very singularity of this landscape that renders futile any attempt to create a realm of Islamic autonomy. Yet it is also this kind of universality that fragments previous forms of Muslim solidarity and collective practice by sub-ordinating them to a single history of the globe. Notions of Islamic universality in the past might have brought the whole world within their compass either by the narrative of conversion, or by linking all its peoples within some hierarchy of God's creation. In both cases Islam still possessed a world—and autonomy—of its own. But as all global movements, from those dedicated to the environment to those devoted to the destruction of atomic weapons so vehemently declare, there exists now only one world in which autonomy is impossible. This is also the world of the jihad. The more traditional forms of Muslim authority are broken down within the jihad, therefore, the more like other global movements such as environmentalism or the anti-globalization protests does Islam become.

Two factors make the jihad into a global movement: the failure of local struggles and the inability to control a global landscape of operations by the politics of intentionality. These factors entail a radical individuation of Islam that is as divorced from modes of collective solidarity and action based on some common history of needs, interests or ideas, as is the individuation of action in other global movements.[33] While I will attend to the nature of this individuation in another chapter, we have already seen how it manifests itself in the extraordinary diversity of the jihad's participants and their lack of cultic uniformity. Given all this, it is hardly surprising that fundamentalists, not to speak of traditional clerical and mystical groups, should vehemently oppose the jihad. So after the attacks of September the eleventh, among a whole host of Muslim objections to these actions from around the world, there was an unprecedented declaration signed by prominent clerics and fundamentalists who included leaders of the Muslim Brotherhood, Hamas and the Jamaat-e Islami:

The undersigned, leaders of Islamic movements, are horrified by the events of Tuesday 11 September 2001 in the United States, which resulted in massive killing, destruction and attack on innocent lives. We express our deepest sympathies and sorrow. We condemn, in the strongest terms, the incidents, which are against all human and Islamic norms. This is grounded in the Noble Laws of Islam, which forbid all forms of attacks on innocents. God Almighty says in the Holy Quran: "No bearer of burdens can bear the burden of another." (Surah al-Isra 17:15)[34]

Since a number of the signatories to this declaration are known neither for their fondness for the United States nor for their abstention from acts of violence against civilians, their protest recognizes the jihad's radical novelty on grounds other than the taking of innocent lives. In fact what is being objected to is not the taking of lives at all but the jihad's globalization beyond a politics of causes and intentions that is organized around shared and therefore very particular histories of needs, interests or ideas. Supporters of the jihad who criticize this position, then, invariably focus on its illogic and hypocrisy in recommending violence is some places but not others. Whatever the future of this struggle, the jihad has stolen the radical edge from fundamentalism, pushing it into an increasingly liberal stance. This has already affected the once "extremist" Muslim Brotherhood and Jamaat-e Islami, as well as the failed revolution of Algeria's Front Islamique du Salut and its military wing, the Groupe Islamique Armée. At the same time as Islamic politics in certain quarters becomes more radical, therefore, it becomes more moderate in others.

2

A DEMOCRATIC HISTORY OF HOLY WAR

The debate on jihad in the Muslim tradition is largely juridical in nature, concentrating upon attempts to define legitimate occasions for holy war, permitted rules of engagement and the like. There is for instance the distinction between the offensive war to spread Islam and the defensive one to protect it, as well as that between the greater or spiritual jihad against one's own evil impulses and the lesser or military jihad against an external enemy. For our purposes, however, what is of chief interest is the fact that this debate, like every legal discussion, is concerned primarily with the privileges of authority——in this case with reserving the jihad's military function for the properly constituted authority of a state.

This exclusive definition of holy war, and its consequently infrequent occurrence (as opposed to what one might call conventional war) in such states, led to a curious situation in the past. On the one hand the religious zeal supposed to mark jihad often remained hidden, given that such holy wars might be linked to, if not altogether displaced by, the desire of princes waging them simply to claim Islamic legitimacy for their houses. On the other hand "conventional war" may have been far more ferocious than the kind of war called "holy". In any case the sort of jihad that was waged by Muslim states into the modern period seems to have been singularly lacking in any special zeal or popular participation.

The jihad today disputes and even mocks the privilege given to authority in this juridical tradition. For instance in this passage from Yahyah bin Ali al-Ghamdi's article "The years of deception", from the ninth issue of the Saudi on-line magazine *Voice of Jihad* that claims to be the mouthpiece of Al-Qaeda in the Arabian Peninsula:

Don't you know that the clerics have stated that *Jihad* becomes a personal duty if the enemy raids the land of the Muslims. [...]? According to those [who disagree with this], a new formula should be put forth. [...] that *Jihad* will become a personal duty when the enemy attacks the land of the Muslims—only if the enemy can be repelled and vanquished, and only if the (Muslim) nation is completely prepared, and only if the ruler—and we don't know who this ruler is—will permit it...[1]

The author's purpose is clear: to wrest the jihad away from the juridical language of the state and make it a strictly individual duty that is more ethical than political in nature. I return below to this widespread rejection by the jihad of the classical doctrine of holy war as a collective or political obligation (*farz kifaya*) similar to that of choosing a ruler or administering justice. One implication of treating holy war as an individual ethical obligation (*farz ayn*), like prayer, is that it becomes spiritualized and finally puts the jihad beyond the pragmatism of political life. So whereas liberal as well as fundamentalist Muslims tried to instrumentalize Islam by attributing social, political or economic functions to its beliefs or practices, the jihad does just the opposite—its task is to de-instrumentalize Islam and make it part of everyday ethics. As Osama bin Laden puts it in the *Ummat* interview:

Al-Qaidah wants to keep jihad alive and active and make it a part of the daily life of the Muslims. It wants to give it the status of worship.[2]

There is, however, a tradition of holy war that does exactly this, one that possesses all the requisite ingredients of religious fervour and popular support, and has, in addition, nothing to do with the juridical politics of a state. Such a tradition of jihad, while it might well have given rise to states, was characteristic of charismatic, mystical and heretical movements, often messianic in nature, located at the peripheries of Islamic power or authority, and frequently directed against them as much as against any infidel presence. It is hardly accidental, therefore, that by far the most popular examples of the *ghazi* or holy warrior in the Muslim world happen to be members of Sufi or mystic fraternities, whose tombs continue to be places of pilgrimage, healing and spiritual succour. Among the most renowned of these saintly warriors was Abdel Kader of the Rif, Sayyid Ahmad Barelvi of the North-West Frontier, Usman dan Fodio of Sokoto, Imam Shamil of Daghestan, Muhammad Ahmad, the Sudanese Mahdi and Sayyid Muhammad, the so-called "Mad Mullah" of Somaliland.

Whether or not these saintly figures participated in any substantial military action, they represent the coalescence of the so-called lesser and greater jihad, where the mystic's spiritual rigour and the warrior's military discipline merge into a single and undifferentiated whole. Among the most fruitful periods for this kind of jihad was that between the eighteenth and twentieth centuries, coinciding exactly with the rise and establishment of European domination over the Muslim world. The most significant of these wars occurred in what are today Chechnya, Afghanistan, Pakistan, India, Saudi Arabia, Sudan, Somalia, Algeria and Nigeria, many of the same places that continue to provide both sites and recruits for the jihad today. Although today's struggles possess causes very different from those of a hundred years ago, these jihads in the Caucasus or Central Asia, the Indian Subcontinent or Northern Africa, provide both Muslims and non-Muslims with most of the terms of debate for today's "holy war".

Tales twice told

While not all jihad movements from the eighteenth to the twentieth centuries were anti-European in character, Western scholars and statesmen took a great interest in them, studying these phenomena in terms that survive to this day. Discussions on jihad in the English language have traditionally focussed on its Indian history, given the extent and importance of their Indian empire for the British. Among the most influential studies of holy war here was the Bengal civilian W. W. Hunter's book of 1871, *The Indian Musulmans: Are They Bound in Conscience to Rebel Against the Queen?* This text, which became prescribed reading for those training for imperial service, was written in response to a question posed by the Viceroy of India, Lord Mayo, that the book repeats in its subtitle.

The Indian Musulmans deals with the famous warrior-martyr Sayyid Ahmad Barelvi, who in the early nineteenth century left India for Afghanistan, where he set up what Hunter describes as a rebel camp that attracted both Afghan and Indian fighters to a jihad initially against the Sikh power centred in the Punjab, and then against their British successors. Rather than being a traditional movement untouched by the West, Sayyid Ahmad's jihad was modern and indeed cosmopolitan in character, a fact to which Hunter's descriptions of its leader's rapturous reception in the British cities of Calcutta and Bombay attest. Similar are his descriptions of the vast and secret network of foreign supporters, financiers and recruits to this Afghan jihad, which engaged the Sikhs, and thereafter the British, in numerous and costly battles in a history that bears an uncanny resemblance to the last Afghan war. Both cases witnessed the establishment of a charismatic foreign leader and his compatriots in Afghanistan, fighting as much against Christian depredations of Muslim lands beyond Afghanistan as against their designs on this country. In both cases the holy war is launched first against one occupying power and then against its successor, which had in fact assisted in the earlier jihad for its own reasons. And in both cases this new power occupied itself with paranoid calculations about international conspiracies against it that included suspects among its own subjects. Given these similarities, it comes as no surprise that Hunter's recommendations to his government should bear a striking resemblance to those bruited about the United States today. These include criticisms of past British policy in the Muslim world, calls for more stringent security and surveillance measures, as well as an emphasis on the reform of Muslim religious and political life, particularly by way of educational institutions.

In fact *The Indian Musulmans* simply assembles European stereotypes about the rebellious nature of Islam, Muslim fanaticism and the political threat of Pan-Islamism into an argument that is ambiguous. Hunter concludes that while British India is not what Islamic jurisprudence would call the *Dar al-Islam* or House of Islam, Muslim rebels are not obliged to rebel against Queen Victoria because the religious freedoms British India offers are such that it cannot be described as the *Dar al-Harb* or House of War either. *The Indian Musulmans*, in other words, is an important work not by reason of its conclusions, but because it highlights both the terms in which Muslim politics are to be considered, and how these are to be analysed. Terms like the House of Islam or the House of War are taken from Muslim juridical literature that often played no role in the actual incidence of holy war, while they are analysed at the level of moral ideas rather than of political or economic interests. Thus Hunter ties jihad to dissent as a moral obligation in a specifically Protestant sense, even using the word conscience for it.

British efforts to grasp jihad in juridical terms were natural enough given their own eminently juridical methods of dealing with it, but they downplayed the local as well as mystical or messianic character of such struggles, thus rendering all debate on holy war universal only through the language of law. This legacy now colours discussion on jihad among both Muslims and non-Muslims. A similar fate awaited British attempts to comprehend jihad by the rhetoric of moral rather than political ideas, which probably resulted from the fact that the European empires were not themselves founded upon conceptions of citizenship, and therefore of the state's foundation in popular consent and representation, but upon moral ideas like the civilizing mission. By their very exclusion from a language of citizenship, the colonies were transformed into landscapes for the working out of moral ideas, as well as of their perversion, in an exemplary way. Such landscapes, popularized by writers like Rudyard Kipling or Joseph Conrad, also provided stages for the re-enactment of Europe's own moral history. Hunter, for example, repeatedly and tiresomely describes the supporters of jihad as Dissenters, Puritans and even Anabaptists. The moderate Muslims of the time are then depicted either as High Church Anglicans who have lost their Protestant zeal or as completely unreformed Roman Catholics. Indeed Hunter cannot help speaking of moderate Muslims in deprecating terms, almost seeming to regret the enmity of the rebels he otherwise scorns:

But important as these [...] sections of the Muhammadans may be from a political point of view, it has always seemed to me an inexpressibly painful incident of our position in India that the best men are not on our side.[3]

At length, however, Hunter recovers both his zeal and fervour for European Christianity in a grand act of iconoclasm and conversion:

We should thus at length have the Muhammadan youth educated upon our own plan. Without interfering in any way with their religion, and in the very process enabling them to learn their religious duties, we should render that religion perhaps less sincere, but certainly less fanatical. The rising generation of Muhammadans would tread the steps which have conducted the Hindus, not long ago the most bigoted nation on earth, into their present state of easy tolerance. Such a tolerance implies a less earnest belief than their fathers had; but it has freed them, as it would liberate the Mussulmans, from the cruelties which they inflicted, the crimes which they perpetrated, and the miseries which they endured, in the name of a mistaken religion. I do not permit myself here to touch upon the means by which, through a state of indifference, the Hindus and Musalmans alike may yet reach a higher level of belief. But I firmly believe that that day will come, and that our system of education, which has hitherto produced only negative virtues, is the first stage towards it. Hitherto the English in India have been but poor iconoclasts after all.[4]

It is remarkable how congruent are the terms of today's debate on the jihad with those of this nineteenth-century work—which is only more honest in pronouncing upon the proselytizing project of the civilizing mission. This explains why current debates on the jihad's legal status, role as a moral obligation for moderate or extreme Muslims, description as an idea linked to the past of the West and possible transformation by education, are in reality all so dated and in fact absurd. These are the very terms, however, that are also taken up and transformed by Muslims of all stripes, in the process making for a truly universal narrative of holy war. Of this a fitting illustration is a Muslim review of Hunter's book written by the important moderate leader Sayyid Ahmad Khan. Sir Sayyid, having invoked the very legalistic conditions for jihad that we have seen the *Voice of Jihad* mock, blames the incidence of holy war against the British on the latter's ignorance about and unequal treatment of Muslims:

The evils that now exist, however, owe their origin greatly to the want of union and sympathy between the rulers and ruled, and ideas like

Dr. Hunter's only tend to widen the gap. I admit that owing to the difference in the mode of life, there is but a limited number of native gentlemen with whom European gentlemen can have cordial intercourse; but this number will, I trust, increase largely every year.[5]

While recommending the inclusion of Muslims into European society upon more or less equal terms as a way of treating with their militancy, Sayyid Ahmad Khan stressed the fact that the gentlemen who deserved such inclusion were to be men like himself, anglicized Muslims who could interpret Islamic passions to the West and European reason to the East. Despite their often sophisticated meditations upon the nature and future of modern Islam, men like Sir Sayyid were forced by political circumstances to play the role merely of intermediaries between Christians and Muslims because none was able to assume political power in his own name. In order to do this Sayyid Ahmad Khan, like his liberal descendants today, who continue to play the same role, also had to emphasize the threatening aspects of an Islamic violence whose substance he was ostensibly denying:

I cannot, however, predict what the actual conduct of the Musalmans would be in the event of an invasion of India by a Mahomedan or any other power. He would be a bold man indeed who would answer for more than his intimate friends and relations, perhaps not even for them. The civil wars in England saw fathers fighting against sons, and brothers against brothers; and no one can tell what the conduct of the whole community would be in any great political convulsion. I have no doubt, but that the Musalmans would do what their political status—favorable or the contrary—would prompt them to do.[6]

These apparently redundant discussions of holy war reveal how the terms in which they were conducted continue, with the necessary stylistic adjustments, to be valid even today. All the usual suspects are already in place: moderate and extremist Muslims, arguments blaming holy war on moral ideas or on the powerlessness of Muslims, the importance of education in creating an interpreter class of liberal Muslims and the like. Indeed these nineteenth-century debates underpin contemporary discussions of the jihad, although they have little if anything to do with it. Yet there is a way in which the jihad tradition of that period between the eighteenth and twentieth centuries does inform its manifestations in our own times, and it is this continuity to which I now turn.

Mystics, heretics and messiahs

In many ways today's jihad builds upon the earlier ventures descri-bed above. It, too, is located on the peripheries of the Muslim world geographically, politically and religiously, operating now in places like Chechnya, Afghanistan, Pakistan and India, as well as in Thai-land and the Philippines. Like its predecessors, the jihad in our times is also peripheral as a set of practices, being charismatic, heretical and even mystical. And like these holy wars of the past, the jihad, too, attempts to move such populist and non-juridical ele-ments to the centre of the Islamic world as part of its struggle. This description runs counter to most academic and journalistic accounts, which derive the jihad from an urban, legalistic and orthodox Muslim tradition originating in the central lands and among the central authorities of Islam and exported to its social and geo-graphical margins by way of preaching and funding.[7]

Notwithstanding my criticisms of genealogical modes of appre-hending the jihad, I do not mean to suggest here that it in fact de-scends in some direct lineage from the holy wars of the eighteenth to twentieth centuries. My point rather is that the jihad's specifically Islamic content draws upon the flotsam and jetsam of received ideas and remembered histories spanning the Muslim tradition that is often received by way of European sources. Of such a tradition these earlier movements form a significant part. This mode of appropriating the past differs from earlier efforts in that it denies the existence of distinct orders or genealogies of Islamic authority. In the past, for example, Sufi ideas and practices were absorbed into the juridical culture of Islam by strengthening and expanding the latter's distinctive order. But with the jihad all such orders and genealogies appear to have broken down, so that its task of synthesis is neither about claiming something from a rival order, nor about setting up or expanding a genealogy of one's own.

Everything we know about Al-Qaeda as a religious movement compares favorably with Sufi or mystical brotherhoods, even if these happen to be disapproved of by members of the movement itself. There is, for instance the very emphasis on jihad, which has historically been a characteristic of Sufi groups. Then there is the cult of martyrs, to whom are attributed supernatural powers including the ability to intercede with God for the salvation of their families, something generally frowned upon by anti-Sufi groups, but advocated by Osama bin Laden himself.[8] Along with these are the jihad's definition as an individual ethical obligation supposedly divorced from the political requirements of a state, as well as a rich and occult world of prophetic and other dreams, which are constantly spoken about within Al-Qaeda. Olivier Roy argues that the individualization of the jihad means that the concern of its advocates with personal faith, repentance and salvation transform their religious practices into those of mysticism.[9]

Apart from the importance of jihad, personal ethics and dreams, we know that Al-Qaeda's leaders are treated by its rank and file as spiritual authorities endowed with a grace that is unrelated to bookish learning of the kind that would mark a traditional cleric or even a fundamentalist. Indeed the Islamic learning of Al-Qaeda's members seems perfunctory at best, the authority of their leaders being vested instead in charisma and experience. If Osama bin Laden, then, is routinely called a *shaykh*, the same title used for Sufi elders, this is not simply because he happens to be a kind of chieftain like the sheikhs of the United Arab Emirates, but because he possesses also a spiritual authority that is manifested in stories of his miraculous preservation from harm and even a prophetic fore-knowledge of events. It is perhaps not accidental that the *kunyah*, or nickname, given Bin Laden within Al-Qaeda is "Abu Abdullah", the Father of Abdullah, which is the same as that given Muhammad. Indeed it is often in these mystical and occult forms that Al-Qaeda's reputation spreads and gains popular appeal, so that we might even consider its jihad to be a manifestation of Sufism, which has been enjoying a global revival of late. This, at least, is what the following passage from William Dalrymple's account of his travels with a Pakistani Muslim suggests:

Halfway along the dangerous road to Kohat—deep in the lawless tribal belt between Pakistan and Afghanistan, and where Osama Bin Laden is widely believed to be sheltering—we passed a small whitewashed shrine that had recently been erected on the side of the road: "That is where the army ambushed and killed two al-Qaeda men escaping from Afghanistan," said Javed Paracha. "Local people soon began to see the two martyrs in their dreams. Now we believe that they are saints. Already many cures and miracles have been reported. If any of our women want to ask anything special from God, they first come here."

He added: "They say that each *shahid* (martyr) emitted a perfume like that of roses. For many days a beautiful scent was coming from the place of their martyrdom."[10]

Mysticism is related to the jihad in its imagery as well as its practices. Unlike the urban world of Muslim law, which was seen in such architectural terms that Islam itself was conceived as a building with five pillars, or as a secure house juxtaposed with the insecure one of war, the landscape of Sufism was dominated by images of caves, ruins and wilderness. These were locations of excess and even disorder that stood in stark contrast to the completely architectonic landscape of a canonical Islam—one that was explicitly tied to political authority. This does not mean that Sufis were themselves disordered and excessive or that they necessarily shunned towns for the countryside, only that mystical brotherhoods laid claim to a landscape of the imagination for whose possession kings were willing to struggle. The imaginative power of this landscape, which has been celebrated in poetry for a millennium now, was taken up and transformed by Muslim movements of all kinds, including today's jihad. The fact that a number of Osama bin Laden's interviews and statements have been filmed in caves, for example, is significant. Apart from their subsequent association with Sufi ascetics (sometimes by way of Buddhist monks, whose cavernous retreats were famous in South and Central Asia as well as in the Near East), caves have a special place in the Quran, most famously the one in which Muhammad first received divine revelation, and the one in which he hid from his persecutors when fleeing Mecca. Then there is the ancient legend of the seven sleepers of Ephesus, which the Quran retells as a story of divine protection from the world's evil. All of these caves are mystic places of refuge removed from the hurly-burly of worldly life.

If an eminent liberal like Sayyid Ahmad Khan had made a pastoral ideal of the disordered mystical landscape, seeing it as a kind of playground for Islam turned into a purely religious identity, fundamentalist eminences like the Pakistani Mawdudi and the Egyptian Sayyid Qutb made it a landscape of exile from an urban order now identified with ideological corruption, or of the new *jahiliyya* (a period of ignorance historically identified with pre-Islamic Arabia), as they called it. But it is the jihad that re-occupies the landscape of Sufism as the site of ethical practice. Conceptually it does this by invoking the doctrine of *hijrat* or migration from lands where Islam is in danger or where its practice is proscribed. While *hijrat* in Muslim juridical literature, as much as in European or American academic writing, is often said to be an alternative to holy war, to be resorted to when the latter's success seems unlikely, its refuge has more often than not become an external base for jihad. Crucial here is the point that the place forsaken is generally the migrant's homeland, while the place of refuge is considered foreign. There are two celebrated instances of such migration in the history of early Islam, one where Muhammad sent some of his followers to Christian Abyssinia for protection, and the other where he had himself to flee his home in Mecca for the town later known as Medina, whose inhabitants came to be called the *ansar*, or helpers.

The terms *hijrat* and *ansar* are important because they continue to be used of events and persons much after the days of the Prophet. In places like the Indian Subcontinent these terms have been used repeatedly, for example to describe the migration of thousands of people to Afghanistan following the First World War. This migration from British territory occurred as the Allied powers were dismantling the defeated Ottoman Empire and occupying the Arabian Peninsula, and thus also the two holy mosques of Mecca and Medina. The similarity of this event, part of an extraordinary agitation known as the Khilafat Movement, with today's concerns about the American occupation of the Arabian Peninsula, is hardly accidental. More famous, however, is the migration of millions of Muslims to the new state of Pakistan following the Partition of India in 1947, the refugees being called *muhajirs*, or migrants. The use of such terms has continued to proliferate in the jihad, with militant outfits named after migrants or helpers, or with the so-called Arab-Afghans being described as migrants and their Taliban hosts as helpers.

The salience of the jihad's use of *hijrat* is that it opens up a whole new landscape for moral action, a wild and disordered landscape distant from the urban centers of juridical Islam—namely the landscape of mysticism and poetry. Indeed there exists a whole aesthetic of such landscapes in the jihad, with the inhospitable and mountainous terrain of the struggles in Chechnya or Afghanistan lovingly described in the photographs and films that promote it, as well as in the descriptions of its fighters themselves. So in a testament posted on the now banned jihad website, www.azzam.com, of one of its reporters killed by an American cluster bomb in the Tora Bora mountains, the physical geography of Afghanistan emerges as a formidable presence. Suraqah Al-Andalusi, or "the Spaniard", his nickname referring to the Muslim kingdom of medieval Andalucia, was probably a British Asian so identified with the Afghan terrain that he literally faded into it in one of his brother's dreams that is described alongside Suraqah's testament:

His brother had a dream, when he came up to someone and asked with great anxiety, "where is my brother [Suraqah]?" The people then pointed to a distant mountain. He asked again, "where is my brother?" and they gave the same response. Then he approached as close as he could get to the mountain and asked again. The people then pointed to a white mountain.[11]

An identification with the wild and disordered places of the Muslim world, which have come to provide the most privileged of arenas for the defense and practice of Islam, is rendered ever more significant when it is matched by an explicit rejection of the traditional centers of Muslim devotion:

The year before his martyrdom, Suraqah decided to make Hajj [the pil-grimage to Mecca] and up to this point, this was the trip that had the most impact on him. Suraqah used to say: "If anyone wonders why the Ummah [Muslim community] is in this bad state, then Hajj will give you the answers." There he saw the ignorance of the Muslims: a people whose tongues were filled with expletives as if they were remembrance duas [prayers], and their failure to understand sharing and generosity when dealing with one another. He saw their innovations and Shirk [associating others with God] when performing the Hajj. He saw outside the Sacred Mosque of Makkah, the interest-based banks in the very same land which 1400 years ago was purified from Shirk by the first group of Muslims led by the Prophet. [...] His blood boiled at how this sacrifice, purchased for the Ummah by the sweat and blood of the Companions [of Muhammad] had been affronted by the establishment of interest-based institutions everywhere. This consolidated his commitment to this path.[12]

This passage suggests nothing so much as the shock of a European Muslim when faced with the Asian and African realities of an Islam he might well have idealized heretofore—a bad tourist experience in the East. But we should not allow ourselves to be detained by the reasons given for Suraqah's disillusionment, including the poor manners of his fellow pilgrims and the presence of interest-based banks in Mecca, both of which might be true and yet perfectly arbitrary at the same time. What is noteworthy is his self-conscious rejection of traditional Islamic centers and authorities, and a corre-sponding glorification of untamed Muslim peripheries as sites for an immeasurably more authentic experience of Islam.

The one element that appears to be missing from this jihad, compared with its predecessors of the eighteenth to the twentieth centuries, is a messianic history. There seem to be no *mahdis* or messiahs either present or expected. On the face of it, this is a remarkable absence given the widespread importance of messianic Islam into the twentieth century—the last Mahdi being a Saudi, one

Muhammad bin Abdullah al-Qahtani, in whose name the Great
Mosque of Mecca was occupied for some two weeks in 1979 by his
brother-in-law Juhayman al-Utaybi and a few hundred men. The
mahdi, who inveighed against the corruption of the monarchy, the
oppression of its people and the degradation of Islam, obviously
enjoyed considerable support among pilgrims in the city, since it
took a great many days for Saudi forces, backed by Pakistani and
French troops, to reclaim Islam's most sacred site amid much
carnage. More importantly, however, the very proclamation of a
mahdi from among a group of men associated with the University of
Medina and its strict Wahhabism, demonstrates the latter's disintegration as the highly legalistic and scripturalist form of Islam it is
meant to be. After all, to acknowledge a *mahdi* is not only to accept
charismatic and indeed mystical authority over that of scriptural
law and its clerical commentators; it is also to fall prey to the very
sort of authority traditionally despised by Wahhabis and strongly
associated with Sufi as well as Shia groups.

While many of Juhayman al-Utaybi's grievances, especially
against the state of things in Saudi Arabia, bear a remarkable resemblance to Osama bin Laden's views, his messianism finds little echo
in Al-Qaeda. What both of these jihads share is their destruction of
the traditional forms and distinctions of Islamic authority, and
indeed the democratization of such authority among all manner of
groups as well as individuals. So perhaps the messiah, too, has fallen
prey to the jihad's democratization and become a collective figure.
In fact there is every reason to think that it is the Muslim community
or *ummah* itself that is meant to serve as the jihad's messiah by rising
up in support of holy war and thus fulfilling its aims. Jean Baudrillard, in his book on the first Gulf War, points out that before the
Muslim community was entrusted with this task, it was the Arab

masses that had been expected by leaders like Saddam Hussein to rise up and rescue them from the overwhelming might of the forces ranged against them.[13] Indeed these forces seem even to have been invited to deploy their might against Arab leaders in order to provoke the grand effect of a popular uprising that never occurred. And in fact how else can overwhelming force be engaged except by a necessarily messianic faith?

Fragments of faith

More startling examples of the jihad's willingness to eschew orthodox in favor of heretical traditions come from its adventurous use of Islamic history, which has been fragmented and almost completely separated from the doctrinal genealogies or ideological orders of the past. Ayman al-Zawahiri, for example, in *Knights Under the Banner of the Prophet*, quotes an interesting passage from Umar Abd al-Rahman, the spiritual leader of the Egyptian Jamaah al-Islamiyyah who is now in an American jail for his role in the World Trade Center bombing of 1993. The context for this quotation is the trial in 1981 of Al-Jihad activists implicated in Egyptian president Sadat's assassination, at which both Zawahiri and Rahman were present:

Shaykh Umar said: "The prosecutor says that those who raise the slogan that power is for God while they themselves want to monopolize power have been described by Muslims and Islamic history as 'Khawarij' (old dissident sect of Islam). Yes, 'power is for God' are words that were previously said by the noble son of Ishaq son of Ya'qub son of Ibrahim: the prophet of God, Yusuf (biblical Joseph), who said those words from his prison in Egypt. The prison's restrictions did not prevent him from saying the words of truth, which were also said by other prophets. Therefore, this is the call of Muslims throughout history. The Khawarij said those words to the fourth orthodox caliph (Ali). If these words were said in the first age (of Islam), those who said them were Khawarij. If they were said in this age, those who said them are Mujahidin".[14]

While Rahman's reference to Joseph in his Egyptian captivity makes the classical comparison between Pharaoh and Sadat by identifying his own imprisoned colleagues with the Hebrew prophet, it is his invocation of the Khawarij that I find far more interesting. The Khawarij or Kharijis, small communities of whom still exist in places like Oman and Zanzibar, were an important group in the history of early Islam, when they were known for supporting the popular removal of any leader who deviated from religiously defined principles of government. It was in part against the simultaneously republican and anarchic politics of the Khawarij that Sunni orthodoxy and its doctrine of the inviolability of political authority were formulated. When the prosecutor in the Sadat assassination trial accused Al-Jihad activists of being like the Khawarij, then, he was speaking with the full weight of Sunni tradition behind him. Shaykh Umar Abd al-Rahman's response, however, welcomed the comparison. Indeed it went so far as to refer favorably to the Khariji opposition to, and eventual assassination of, the fourth caliph Ali, who was also Muhammad's cousin and son-in-law. By implication, the assassinated Sadat is here being compared to the eminently orthodox figure of Ali, and Al-Jihad militants to his assassins.

By quoting this remarkable statement from the Sadat assassination trial, Ayman al-Zawahiri seems deliberately to be drawing attention to the unorthodox and iconoclastic nature of the jihad. This should not, however, be interpreted in any way as indicating the jihad's wholesale support of a Khariji position, or its rejection of Ali's authority and religious status. It indicates rather the fact that Islamic history and authority has been completely disaggregated and is no longer clustered within more or less distinct lineages of doctrine or ideology that can be identified with particular groups.

So Rahman and Zawahiri are free to glorify the Khawarij and cas-
tigate Ali at one point but might well reverse this evaluation at
another. In effect all traditional forms of intellectual and political
grouping or identification have been fragmented, their elements
scattered like debris for the picking, to be recycled in ever more
temporary constructions.[15] This is what gives Al-Qaeda its flexi-
bility both religiously and politically, allowing Zawahiri, for instance, to assign Shia Iran and secular Turkey prominent roles in his
vision of Islam's geo-political freedom.[16]

This breakdown of Islamic authority through the dispersal and
recycling of its historical representations has very little if anything
to do with tolerance as a liberal virtue. It has just as little to do with
pragmatic politics. Instead the jihad's catholic approach to the
variety of Islamic traditions signals a democratization of authority in
the Muslim world, though without in the least precluding hostility
among its various factions. As an explicitly Sunni enterprise, the
jihad's dealings with Shiism are exemplary in showing how this
democratization of authority might operate alongside disagreement
and recrimination. The jihad is indebted to Shiism for much of its
lexicon and even practice. Martyrdom, for instance, while not being a
specifically Shiite doctrine or practice, is very strongly associated
with it. Suicide bombing and the whole rhetoric of the martyrdom
operation enters the jihad from Iran's conduct of its decade-long
war with Iraq, as well as from Hezbollah's operations against the
Israelis in Lebanon, from which Hamas has quite explicitly taken
it up.

Shiite themes have been present within militant Sunnism for
some time now. Revolutionary Iran, for example, not only gal-
vanized Muslim politics throughout this world, but also gained the
support of the most militant elements within it. Similarly the
Ayatullah Khomeini's fatwa against Salman Rushdie, which in 1989

transformed the congeries of protests against *The Satanic Verses* among Indian, Pakistani and British Muslims into Islam's first global movement, ended up being acknowledged by militant groups like Islamic Jihad in Palestine and the Jamaah al-Islamiyya of Egypt. Deploying the same strategy as they had during the Islamic Revolution in 1979, less radical Sunni groups refused to accept the authority of a Shiite like Khomeini and deprecated what they saw as his misuse of a legal opinion like the fatwa, which was made into a verdict outside its traditional jurisdiction. Bizarrely the Rushdie Affair became Islam's first global movement by reversing the stereotyped juxtaposition of a secular West and a religious East. Only Western commentators saw *The Satanic Verses* controversy in religious terms. For Khomeini and his militant Sunni supporters, the issue was entirely secular, about the representation of Muhammad as a leader, husband and family man. Protesters against the novel were demanding for their Prophet the same recognition and respect that Rushdie himself had championed in the form of multiculturalism.[17]

But the role of Shiism in the jihad goes well beyond the facts of Iran's revolution and even of its Ithnaashari form. So the word *fedayeen*, or devotees, is used for their fighters by several Sunni groups, though it takes its radical aspect from the Ismaili form of Shiism. An Ismaili group of the Middle Ages, the so-called Assassins, was famous for suicide missions conducted by such devotees. One of the suicide bombers of 9/11, Khalid al-Mihdhar, was nicknamed Sinan within Al-Qaeda, the name here probably referring to Rashid al-Din Sinan, the Assassin leader in Syria also known as the Old Man of the Mountain. The infiltration into the jihad of Shiite terms and practices does not make for a commonality of ideas or interests between any Sunni and Shia group—on the contrary. This infiltration is not the result of some effort at religious alliance-

building or even synthesis, but is due rather to the jihad's fragmentation of traditional Muslim forms of authority and the re-use of
their elements in the most diverse ways.

Al-Qaeda leaders like Osama bin Laden or Ayman al-Zawahiri
have never been known either to preach or practice anti-Shia
politics, indeed the opposite, with Bin Laden repeatedly urging
Muslims to ignore internal differences and even appearing to
uphold the Islamic credentials of Shiite Iran by comparing the
longed-for ouster of the Saudi monarch to the expulsion of the
Shah.[18] *The 9/11 Commission Report* even suggests links between Al-
Qaeda, Hezbollah and Iran.[19] In fact Bin Laden is not averse to
claiming the support not only of heretics for the jihad, but of
apostates as well, as he does in his celebrated declaration of war
against the United States in 2001:

If it is not possible to push back the enemy except by the collective
movement of the Muslim people, then there is a duty on the Muslims to
ignore the minor differences among themselves; the ill effect of ignoring
these differences, at a given period of time, is much less than the ill effect of
the occupation of the Muslims' land by the main Kufr [infidel]. Ibn
Taymiyya had explained this issue and emphasized the importance of
dealing with the major threat [sic.] on the expense of the minor one. He
described the situation of the Muslims and the Mujahideen and stated that
even the military personnel who are not practicing Islam are not exempted
from the duty of Jihad against the enemy.[20]

While Bin Laden's recommendation to ignore internal differences
among Muslims is meant to be temporary, given the nature of the
war he contemplates, this hiatus could well extend for decades if
not centuries, thus indicating only a will to defer rather than resolve
such conflicts. Many of the groups affiliated with Al-Qaeda in
Pakistan and Afghanistan, however, entertain no such qualms about
sectarian strife. In these areas, where distrust between Sunni and

Shia has a long history, the language and tactics of the jihad, for example suicide bombing, are also being used against Shiites. Mariam Abou Zahab has pointed out that explicitly anti-Shia groups like the Sipah-e Sahaba (Soldiers of the Prophet's Companions) or the Jaish-e Muhammad (Muhammad's Army) in Pakistan were weaned away from a local politics of sectarian militancy and into the larger struggle of the jihad by Al-Qaeda, but this respite seems not to have lasted.[21] Instead Shiites have now become the jihad's enemies alongside India, Israel or the United States, rather than representing merely local nuisances for these Pakistani outfits. Anti-Shia violence in Pakistan is paradoxically linked to the Sunni cultivation of Shiite beliefs and practices, part of what I refer to as the jihad's democratization of Islam, in which the fragmentation of traditional authority and the resulting openness to new beliefs and practices facilitate the possibility of sectarian amity as much as of enmity.

The love that dare not speak its name

With the incorporation of anti-Shia violence into the global landscape of the jihad it, too, has ceased being a part simply of local politics. After all the frequent killings of Shiites in Pakistan no longer have any old-fashioned rationality attached to them, because they are increasingly divorced from particular persons, places and events—for instance the Shia commemorations of Muharram that had formerly provided the chief occasion for sectarian violence. These killings now possess no particularity of time or place, reason or target, but have become generalized and therefore abstract in their violence. So Muhammad Qasim Zaman, who in his book *The Ulama in Contemporary Islam* very helpfully summarizes the would-be causes of Pakistani sectarianism, ends up with a laundry list of variegated items that cannot provide it any political rationality. This list includes "catalysts" of violence like the successful agitation of the 1970s to declare a group called the Ahmadis non-Muslim, which provided both a precedent and an example for anti-Shia militancy, as well as the increasing assertiveness of Shiites themselves following Iran's revolution in 1979. These catalysts apart, Zaman attributes the rise of Pakistani sectarianism to Sunni resentment of Shia landowners in parts of the Punjab, to the rise and consolidation along sectarian lines of a Sunni middle class in the same province, to the return and re-integration also along sectarian lines of migrant labor from the Persian Gulf, and to Sunni groups striving to dominate their peers by propagating anti-Shia activities.[22]

True though they all might be, Zaman recognizes that such varying causes do not add up to a convincing explanation of sectarianism in Pakistan, not least because many of them, such as the influence of Iran's Islamic Revolution and the consequent rise of Shia assertiveness world-wide, ceased to be relevant as factors a long time ago. And with the absence of Shia aggressiveness, Zaman's remaining causes cease to reflect any political rationality, Shiism having been transformed into a purely symbolic factor in the constitution of Sunni militancy. Only the odd instances of exploitation by Shia landlords remain as properly political causes for Pakistani sectarianism, but they can hardly account for its widespread character. The Shiites, after all, pose no threat to Sunnis in political, economic or demographic terms, although they do form majorities in some parliamentary constituencies, and there have been incidents of conversion to Shiism in the Punjab, as there have been to Ahmadism and Christianity in the same province. A few prominent landowners such as the Bhuttos in Sindh and some families of the Punjab are also Shiites. It might be true that the death of certain Shia landowners, businessmen or professionals might benefit their Sunni laborers, clients or rivals, just as the death of any person might satisfy an enemy, but these purely material benefits cannot account for the widespread and indiscriminate nature of the killing, to say nothing of the rhetoric that accompanies it.[23]

In fact the nature and scale of this violence bear little relation to traditional prejudices or animosities between Sunnis and Shiites in the Indian subcontinent, whose violent episodes were in any case confined to particular persons, places and events, thus possessing political rationality of an old fashioned sort.[24] Violence against the Shia in Pakistan is new not only because it is indiscriminate, but also because it is organized by the Sipah-e Sahaba and Jaish-e Muhammad. In addition to fighting the jihad in Afghanistan and India, these groups are dedicated to defending Sunnism against what they see as Shiite obstinacy, malignity and, very importantly, seduction, since the Shia are considered dangerous because of the very attraction they pose for Sunnis. While it is often pointed out that this new kind of violence emerged after the Islamic Revolution in Iran, perhaps more important is the fact that its protagonists received arms, training and legitimacy during the anti-Soviet jihad in Afghanistan, a by-product of which was the militarization of Pakistani society as a whole. The Shia for their part did not suffer these attacks uncomplainingly but instead retaliated in equal measure. Given the size, numbers and resources of the militias arrayed against them, however, often with support from the Pakistani state, the one or two Shiite forces backed by Iran were always insignificant in comparison.

If the Iranian revolution and subsequent efflorescence of Shia radicalism worldwide acted as a spur to sectarian violence among Sunnis, this was not because Pakistani Shiites had become particularly treacherous or even anti-Sunni. Indeed the contrary is probably true, since the Islamic Revolution was ostentatiously ecumenical and sought agreement among radical movements all over the Muslim world, also supporting the struggles of Sunni populations like the Palestinians or Bosnians. And while these maneuvers no doubt had political aims that favored Iran, they offered no real threat to the Sunni world—indeed we have seen how the Islamic Revolution actually enjoyed the support of some among the most militant Sunni groups. At best, then, Iran was only one among many possible backers, like the United States or the Soviet Union, of revolutionary change in the Muslim world—as demonstrated most famously in Afghanistan's complicated proxy wars. So it was perhaps because Shiism had come to support rather than oppose certain forms of Sunni militancy that it was seen as a threat, which in effect means that the more Sunni radicalism adopted Shia terms and practices, the more anti-Shia it became. In Pakistan anti-Shia militancy is characterized by the veneration of Sunni martyrs in very Shiite ways that include ritual mourning, as well as by the extensive and equally Shiite use of religious dissimulation for reasons like preaching, protection and even attack, since the Sunni suicide bombers who blow themselves up in Shia mosques do so while pretending to be Shiite worshippers. These were the very practices that had in the past provided the basis for Sunni polemics against the Shia.

Paradoxically, smaller Shia communities like the Nizari and Mustaalavi Ismailis, who are in both their beliefs and practices far more heretical by Sunni standards than the Shia Ithnaasharis, have yet to become the targets of much sectarian violence. This is odd given the fact that these very exclusive groups are often highly visible in their appearance, language or prosperity, and, in places like the Northern Areas of Pakistan form sizeable and even majority populations. While they generally eschew politics and have no foreign government like that of Iran backing them, these groups not only enjoy the patronage and goodwill of "enemy" countries like India or the United States, but also line up alongside the West against jihadi movements and regimes such as the Taliban. The Ismailis by no means meet with the approval of Sunni sectaries, and have been vilified and harassed by them, but they are unlikely to become more than casual victims of the jihad because they do not in fact share very much with Sunnis, or rather do not compete with them over the same terms and practices. They are, in other words, relatively protected from sectarian violence by virtue of their very differences, as well as because they have nothing to offer Sunni militancy, a few antiquarian symbols apart—although this situation might change given the gravitation towards liberal forms of Sunnism by Ismaili communities that seek wider acceptability in the Muslim world. The only kind of Shiism that meets with regular and systematic Sunni disapproval, therefore, is the one closest to it. Indeed in this sense Sunni quarrels with the Shia are more like their disputes with each other, say between the Deobandi and Barelvi schools, as well as with the Ahmadis, whose practices are also very close to Sunni ones, rather than being reminiscent of their fight against Christians, Hindus or Ismailis, to say nothing of Zoroastrians or Sikhs, who seem to enjoy complete immunity from attack.

It is as if the new universality of Shia themes, or their democratization within Sunni circles, suddenly made the continued separateness of Shiism seem like an affront. This may be why Sunni polemic in Pakistan no longer castigates Shiism for its different beliefs and practices, emphasizing instead the dangers of its very similarity to Sunnism. Indeed traditional points of contention between the sects, focusing on differences in the postures and rituals of prayer, to say nothing of differences in the apostolic succession, have effectively vanished from this polemic. Abandoning the kind of theological argumentation that would dispute such Shiite differences by reference to sacred and other authoritative texts, groups like the Sipah-e Sahaba seem more inclined to accuse the Shia of betraying the very things they hold in common with Sunnis. This they are meant to do by revering their imams above Muhammad, by demeaning the Prophet in their insulting references to certain of his relatives and companions, and by casting doubts on the authenticity of the Quran. These are all hackneyed accusations, but they seem to be deployed in a new way, in which it is no longer the differences of Shia belief or practice that are a problem, mistaken though these might well be, but the allegation that Shiites are unfaithful to the very Prophet, scripture and religion they hold in common with Sunnis. Much Sunni resentment may be due to the fact that Shiite abuses cannot be reciprocated in kind, since the latter's imams were themselves close relatives of the Prophet and so already part of Sunnism, posing therefore a kind of threat from within—the Trojan horse of Shiism. This is why the task of a group like the Sipah-e Sahaba is to accentuate rather than diminish Shia differences by having them declared a non-Muslim minority—since it is their similarity to Sunnism and not difference from it that poses a problem.

Militant Sunnism has abandoned the theological disputes of the past, based as these were on differing claims to the truth, and adopted a democratic narrative of enmity instead. By this I mean that it is no longer arguments about truth that animate such militants, only a desire for the recognition and respect of their neighbors, who are accused of insulting their sanctities while at the same time claiming to be fellow Muslims. Like multiculturalists elsewhere, all these militants say they want is equal recognition and equal respect.[25] And about this they are not altogether wrong, since

Sunni polemic in Pakistan is marked by its very desire for the thing it hates. Not only does it adopt practices heretofore reviled as Shia, like the veneration of holy personages, but is characterized by a sentimental narrative of insulted pride and injured feelings that seems to ask for nothing more than Shia solicitude. Indeed this polemic's concern with seduction and betrayal makes lovers of the Shia rather than rivals, since it demands nothing less than fidelity from them. It is the love that dare not speak its name. Premised upon the putative brotherhood of all Muslims, the sentimental narrative of Sunni militancy claims to desire only communion with the Shia, and makes good this claim by its fragmentation of Islam's traditional orders and genealogies, and the democratic dispersal of their various elements. Could it be, then, that Shiism poses a problem for this narrative because it is imagined as a form of Muslim authority, and of practice, that has not yet been broken down, democratized and thus rendered universal in the accommodating bosom of militant Sunnism?

3

MONOTHEISTIC GEOGRAPHIES

As we have seen, the jihad abandons the authorities and heartlands of Islam by taking to the peripheries, assuming there a charismatic, mystical and even heretical countenance that dismembers the old social and religious distinctions of Islam. But the jihad also infiltrates these central lands and authorities from the peripheries, thereby disaggregating their very centrality to democratize Islam and disperse it globally. The fate of the Middle East as a site that is supposedly central to Islam illustrates well how this process occurs.

Ayman al-Zawahiri is exemplary here not only because he abandoned the struggle in Egypt for that in Afghanistan, but also because he deliberately renounced regional struggles altogether for the global jihad. Zawahiri's reasoning for this dual abandonment was a very simple one: the failure of jihad as a regional enterprise, especially in the Middle East. This is how, for instance, he describes its particularly Egyptian failure in *Knights Under the Banner of the Prophet*:

The problem of finding a secure base for jihad activity in Egypt used to occupy me a lot, in view of the pursuits to which we were subjected by the security forces and because of Egypt's flat terrain which made government control easy, for the River Nile runs in its narrow valley between two deserts that have no vegetation or water. Such a terrain made guerrilla warfare in Egypt impossible and, as a result, forced the inhabitants of this valley to submit to the central government and be exploited as workers and compelled them to be recruited in its army.[1]

This is a classical analysis of political control and resistance in the Nile valley, as true of modern as it was of ancient Egypt. Muslim struggles in Egypt took on a peculiar form that Zawahiri describes thus:

[T]he outlet for pent-up resentment was the explosions that occurred at infrequent intervals just like an extinct volcano that no one knows when it will erupt, or like an earthquake that no one knows when it will shake the ground with all that lies on it. It was not strange, therefore, that the history of the contemporary Islamist movement since the 1940's has been one of repeated crackdowns by the authorities.[2]

Despite his bleak assessment of the jihad in Egypt, Zawahiri insists that it is here, in the most important country of the Middle East, where holy war must return to conquer. His colleague Osama bin Laden, naturally, opts for his own homeland, the Arabian Peninsula, which just goes to show how unimportant is doctrinal uniformity to the jihad. The important point about this rather partisan and even unrealistic position (given his pronouncements on the futility of the struggle in Egypt) is not Zawahiri's patriotism so much as the way in which he relates the jihad at home to that abroad. Here, then, are Zawahiri's reasons for going to Afghanistan:

My connection with Afghanistan began in the summer of 1980 by a twist of fate, when I was temporarily filling in for one of my colleagues at Al-Sayyidah Zaynab Clinic, which was administered by the Muslim Brotherhood's Islamic Medical Society. One night the clinic director, a Muslim Brother, asked me if I would like to travel to Pakistan to contribute, through my work as a surgeon, to the medical relief effort among the Afghan refugees. I immediately agreed because I saw this as an opportunity to get to know one of the arenas of jihad that might be a tributary and base for jihad in Egypt and the Arab region, the heart of the Islamic world, where the basic battle of Islam was being fought.[3]

Zawahiri, the man who abandoned struggle in Egypt for the jihad elsewhere, and who also became notorious for supporting a global rather than regional holy war, is by no means lacking in national feeling and even Arab pride. But no one would suggest that by adopting the global over some regional position one becomes absolutely neutral with respect to all localities. On the contrary, the adoption of a global perspective might just as well lead to the intensification of national or linguistic chauvinism, but only in a completely fragmented geo-political landscape where centres and peripheries seem almost to have changed places. So we know that there was not much love lost between Arab fighters and their Afghan hosts, who were often viewed by the former as little more than savages. But these very Arabs also tended to take Afghan wives, learn local languages and dress in a curious mixture of Middle Eastern and South or Central Asian clothing. There is no contradiction here because such integration did not represent pan-Islamic unity so much as the opposite—Islam's geo-political fragmentation.

In the passage quoted above, Ayman al-Zawahiri is adamant that the jihad, instead of being exported from the centre to the periphery, will be imported from the periphery to the centre. And this immediately puts the idea of a centre itself in doubt by robbing it of one of its most important attributes—the ability to expand. Suddenly, then, the jihad as one of the most vital functions of Islam has to be brought into the Middle East from the outside, rather than moving outward from this central place. Zawahiri proffers several reasons for the superiority of the Afghan jihad over similar struggles in the Arab world. For one thing, it provided a kind of laboratory in which holy war might be developed into a global phenomenon:

A jihadist movement needs an arena that would act like an incubator where its seeds would grow and where it can acquire practical experience in combat, politics and organizational matters.[4]

More than this, however, it is the struggle in these very peripheries that exhibit Islam's purity in the most uncompromising of ways:

The Muslim youths in Afghanistan waged the war to liberate Muslim land under purely Islamic slogans, a very vital matter, for many of the liberation battles in our Muslim world had used composite slogans, that mixed nationalism with Islam and, indeed, sometimes caused Islam to intermingle with leftist, communist slogans. This produced a schism in the thinking of the Muslim young men between their Islamic jihadist ideology that should rest on pure loyalty to God's religion, and its practical implementation.[5]

While Zawahiri criticizes the ideologies of the Cold War, whose presence in the Middle East he claims had only muddied the waters of Muslim struggles, he is not above making use of them himself. But then it isn't easy to take leave of old-fashioned politics by forsaking nationalism and communism only to retain the concept of ideology that is fundamental to both. Apart from its value as a laboratory of the jihad and its Islamic purity, the war in Afghanistan was important to the Arab world for two additional reasons—the first being that it had a global significance which conflicts in the Middle East simply did not:

A further significant point was that the jihad battles in Afghanistan destroyed the myth of a (superpower) in the minds of the Muslim mujahidin young men. The USSR, a superpower with the largest land army in the world, was destroyed and the remnants of its troops fled Afghanistan before the eyes of the Muslim youths and as a result of their actions.[6]

Second, it was in Afghanistan, rather than in a place like Egypt, that the global character of Islam became evident in the sheer diversity of Muslims participating in the jihad:

It also gave young Muslim mujahidin—Arabs, Pakistanis, Turks and Muslims from Central and East Asia—a great opportunity to get acquainted with each other on the land of Afghan jihad through their comradeship-at-arms against the enemies of Islam.[7]

I have quoted Zawahiri here to show how, despite the importance he attaches to the jihad in the central lands of the Middle East, it is in fact on the Central and South Asian periphery that holy war achieves its purest Islamic form. Traditional notions of centres and peripheries in the Muslim world, whether of geography or authority, have broken down in the jihad to the extent of becoming quite nonsensical.

Zawahiri's refrains about the importance of Egypt to the jihad, then, are curious neither because of their nationalist sentiment, nor because they overestimate the significance of the Arab world for global Islam. The Middle East is undeniably significant to the Muslim world as a whole, though perhaps more for geo-political than strictly religious reasons. What is puzzling about Zawahiri's remarks are his attempts to constitute the Arab world anew within a landscape where Islamic authority as well as geography have been completely dispersed. And it is to this dispersal and reconstitution that I now turn. The Humpty-Dumpty of the Middle East is put back together in the jihad not as a site of historical or contemporary religious authority, let alone of Islamic political power, but instead as the symbolic battlefield of the three monotheisms, something which in any case it had already become in the world of Euro-American journalism and popular culture. The Middle East enjoys this specifically metaphysical status in the jihad.

Mirages of the Middle East

What exactly is the Middle East, or the Arab world, which is often seen as its analogue? Is it the absence or presence of Israel, Turkey, Iran or even North Africa that marks the distinction between the two? A language, especially a sacred and formerly imperial one like Arabic, cannot be identified with or confined to a specific region.

As one of the major vehicles for Islamic practice around the world, used in ritual forms by millions who comprehend almost nothing of it, Arabic not only moves beyond regional boundaries but also transforms the places in which it is uttered. These places where Arabic is spoken come therefore to represent an Islamic universality that extends to the furthest reaches of the globe. In other words the Arabic language, as much as any region defined as its site of origin, are inherently unstable categories. Rather than constituting imperial centres whose culture is spread across a vast hinterland, both the Arabic language and the region called Arab, neither of which possesses any political dominance in the larger Muslim world, represent a universality that constantly threatens its own linguistic and geographical bases.

This universality is made startlingly visible in the holy cities scattered over the Middle East, which have had shifting and cosmopolitan populations of both permanent residents and visiting pilgrims for centuries. Cities like Mecca and Medina in Saudi Arabia, as well as the Shia centres of Najaf and Karbala in Iraq, have not only entertained many foreign Muslims, but have also come to be dependent on them in economic and religious terms. In addition to being sites of international commerce and habitation, these holy cities became recipients of monetary gifts and large public works projects funded by foreign Muslims that have gone so far as to alter their religious importance. Juan Cole, for instance, points out that it was Indian money and pilgrims during the eighteenth and nineteenth centuries that made Najaf and Karbala into important sites of pilgrimage and religious authority for Shiites around the world.[8]

Like Rome and Jerusalem, the holy cities of the Muslim Middle East have achieved the kind of religious universality that makes it difficult for them to be circumscribed within entirely regional, not to mention national, geographies. We know, for instance, that despite all its attempts to do so, the House of Saud has never managed to claim Mecca and Medina as its own patrimony. Indeed the title which is meant to give the Saudi king a peculiar Islamic legitimacy, that of being the Servant of the Two Holy Places, seems to have worked more against him than otherwise, for even conceptually it subordinates his country and its sovereignty to an Islamic universality over which he has very little if any control. From Iranian demonstrations and Wahhabi gun-battles in the area around the great mosque of Mecca, to more recent demands by Al-Qaeda that the two sacred cities be freed from the Saudi monarchy, the very universality of these holy places pushes them beyond any linguistic or geographical particularity.

Even without these sacred sites, the Arab world, and the Middle East with which it is often conflated, come across as fairly ramshackle entities. After all there exist areas like Spain which were once part of the Arab world but are no longer, people like the Berbers in Algeria, the Circassians in Jordan or the Kurds in Iraq who belong in the Arab world and even speak Arabic but who are not accounted Arabs, African groups in countries like Mauritania who speak Arabic but do not belong in the Arab world, and religious groups like Christians in Lebanon who speak Arabic and are considered Arabs but happen not to be Muslims. In other words the categories Arab or Middle Eastern have little if any consistency. Being made up of an arbitrary and vacillating congeries of language, religion and race, such categories have only temporary meaning, and this, too, only in terms of a global politics that is frequently determined outside the region's linguistic as well as geographical borders.

As a geographical entity the Middle East, or the Arab world, is probably a secularized name for Christianity's Holy Land. It is this land whose terrain has been so lovingly imagined in Christian art and literature down the ages as a true geography, the place where Jesus walked, instead of as a sacred city like Jerusalem or a set of sacred sites like Temple Mount or the Church of the Holy Sepulchre. These latter were more architectural than geographical in nature.[9] The geography of the Holy Land was subsequently adopted by Jewish thought in Europe, finally coming to be defined by the state of Israel and its close neighbours. Indeed categories like the Middle East are often invoked primarily in terms of the Israeli-Palestinian conflict, which is then transformed into an Arab-Jewish struggle.[10] The cause of Palestine has assumed its remarkable symbolic value for Muslims on the same model as the Christian-Jewish Holy Land, and specifically as that site where the three monotheisms engage in a conflict that is as much metaphysical as political.

Ayman al-Zawahiri, along with the global jihad more generally, recognizes the symbolic and even imaginary role played by the Palestinian cause in the constitution of the Middle East, or of the Arab world, as a geographical as well as a religious entity. In seeking to mobilize Muslim populations around the world by invoking the Palestinian cause, Zawahiri has the following to say about it:

The strange thing is that secularists, who brought disasters to the Muslim nation, particularly on the arena of the Arab-Israeli conflict; and who started the march of treason by recognizing Israel beginning with the Armistice Agreement of 1949, as we explained earlier, are the ones who talk the most about the issue of Palestine.[11]

Stranger still is the fact that the Muslims, who have sacrificed the most for Jerusalem, whose doctrine and Shari'ah (law) prevent them from abandoning any part of Palestine or recognizing Israel, as we explained earlier; and who are the most capable of leading the nation in its jihad against Israel are the least active in championing the issue of Palestine and raising its slogans among the masses.[12]

Osama bin Laden is, if anything, even more outspoken not only about the symbolic value of the Palestinian cause, but about its fluctuating or intermittent popularity as well. In fact he is forthright in refusing to recognize a hierarchy of priorities for the jihad based on anything but strategic considerations. As far as Bin Laden is concerned a cause like the Palestinian one must be subordinated to the jihad as a global struggle. And in the Middle East this struggle is not simply about the political, economic or religious freedom of Muslim lands but rather about something metaphysical, what the jihad never tires of describing as the conflict between Muslims, Christians and Jews—the three monotheistic faiths. So when it was pointed out to him by the Al-Jazeera correspondent Tayseer Alouni, during an interview in October of 2001, that his spate of references to the Palestinian struggle were relatively new, Bin Laden responded in the following manner:

Jihad is a duty to liberate Al-Aqsa [the Dome of the Rock mosque in Jerusalem], and to help the powerless in Palestine, Iraq and Lebanon and in every Muslim country. There is no doubt that the liberation of the Arabian Peninsula from infidels is a duty as well. But it is not right to say that Osama put the Palestinian issue first. I have given speeches in which I encourage Muslims to boycott America economically. I said Americans take our money and give it to Israel to kill our children in Palestine. I established a front a few years ago named The Islamic Front for Jihad against the Jews and the Crusaders. Sometimes we find the right elements to push for one cause more than the other. Last year's blessed intifada helped us to push more for the Palestinian issue. This push helps the other cause. Attacking America helps the cause of Palestine and vice versa. No conflict between the two; on the contrary, one serves the other.[13]

Oil, therefore, might well be a more important factor for the peace, stability and future of the Middle East than the Palestinian cause, something that supporters of the jihad acknowledge, but without forgetting meanwhile that it is the symbolic plight of the Palestinians that will ensure the widest support if it is completely translated into the terms of global Islam. This is not to suggest that the Palestinian cause has no importance of its own, only that it has far greater weight as a factor in the imaginary constitution of the Middle East as a Holy Land, and now possibly of the Muslim world as an extended figure of such a Holy Land. It is not accidental that elements of the Christian-Jewish Holy Land, which underpin the Middle East or Arab world as a category, have become evident not only in Muslim glorifications of Jerusalem or of the Palestinians as a victimised people, but also in the jihad's definition of the Arabian Peninsula and its sacred sites as a Holy Land to be freed from alien occupation. While there is some precedent for such a definition, I contend that its contemporary landscape is quite new, divorced as it is from any traditional vision of a political order such as the caliphate.

Nothing, however, illustrates the recent and symbolic constitution of the Middle East for modern politics, and especially for the politics of Islam, than the fact that this category did not exist till the end of the First World War. Before this, the Arab world enjoyed neither unity nor autonomy, being, for the most part, an Ottoman possession. As a portion of the Ottoman Empire the Middle East formed part of the same political order as Southern Europe, both being ruled from Constantinople, a city that was the capital of the caliphate and therefore by rights the true centre of the Muslim world. It is only after the dismemberment of the Ottoman Empire that both the Middle East and its autonomous status as the Holy Land of monotheism come into being. It is of little relevance whether this Holy Land is confined to the sacred mosques of Jerusalem, Mecca and Medina or includes these cities in their entirety, whether it is confined within the political boundaries of Israel-Palestine and Saudi Arabia or includes larger territories in the region. Rather, it is the idea of the Holy Land that gives the Middle East what meaning it has as an Islamic entity—this is why identifying its territory by the names of these great mosques is so important for the jihad.

The cosmopolitan militant

The Middle East today is a truly dispersed entity, with much of its press headquartered in London, its language used by Arab and non-Arab alike, and even its jihad originating elsewhere. Indeed the Middle East might well be grounded in a specific territory only by its oil wells, which, as Jacques Derrida suggests while reflecting on the attacks of 9/11, "remain among the rare territories left, among the last nonvirtualizable terrestrial places."[14] But even here it disintegrates. The oil-rich kingdoms of the Persian Gulf, for example, which play such a large role in the jihad, from providing it funds to homes and constituencies, were initially created, governed and exploited by British imperialism in the form of the Government of India. It was this government and its Indian subjects that founded, managed and manned the oil industries of these countries, including Iraq, till well after the end of British rule in 1947.

Even today this area is linked demographically, economically and culturally more to the Indian Subcontinent, South-East Asia and East Africa than it is to the rest of the Middle East. So apart from the large foreign populations settled in these monarchies, sometimes forming the majority of their inhabitants, many of the historical centres in this extended region owe their existence to commercial links with Asia and Africa. Aden, for instance, from whence Osama Bin Laden's family originated (his father leaving this declining city for new opportunities in Saudi Arabia), was an important place in its time only because it served as a link in the British route to and from India, also possessing, therefore, a large Indian population. Aden, indeed, was in some ways the Dubai of its time—a cosmopolitan city more similar in every way to Bombay or London than to the Yemeni capital of Sana. This is why the common description of the Bin Laden family as Yemeni is as much correct as it is not.

But the relationship between the Persian Gulf and points south or east of it is not all one-way. This small region provides a huge country like India, for example, with the bulk of its foreign invest-ment, mostly in the form of remittances from Indians settled there, keeps its national airline financially viable by ferrying Indians to and from various sheikhdoms, and acts as a major centre both for its entertainment industry and crime syndicates. Given all this, it should come as no surprise if a Christian migrant from the Indian state of Kerala were to be far more integrated and at home in a place like Dubai than a Muslim migrant from Morocco who is Arabic-speak-ing to boot. After all, one is as likely to encounter Urdu or Swahili in public places here as one is of encountering Arabic.

Most important in its fragmentation as a Middle Eastern region, however, is the fact that the Persian Gulf's disparate populations are not linked by any relations, whether social, political or economic, that happen to be based on citizenship. Since foreigners here tend to have no rights of permanent residence, let alone equal rights with those defined as indigenes, who themselves are by no means equal citizens of nation states, all relations among these populations tend to be cosmopolitan instead of national. The moment citizenship rights are denied to a segment of a state's population, especially an enormous population like that of foreigners in the Gulf, citizenship itself disappears as an aspect of national uniformity, along with all notions of a common culture and solidarity. The end result is perhaps a kind of market managed by rules that have nothing to do with political representation or participation as we recognize them.

This curious world, which may function in various forms within immigrant and other cosmopolitan enclaves elsewhere, seems to mirror rather closely the world of the jihad itself. It is, after all, the world of the global marketplace, and includes within its ambit not only multi-national corporations or trans-national trading networks, but also the international students, economic migrants, illegal aliens and political refugees who form part and parcel of these commercial enterprises. And we know that the global transactions of the jihad, along with its incredibly mobile operators, use and indeed emerge from such networks and enclaves, in which an old-fashioned politics of intentionality and collective mobilization based on some common need, interest or idea has been ruled out. One has only to consider the remarkable peregrinations of the 9/11 hijackers, running the gamut from German universities and Afghan training camps to American flight schools, and passing through the immigrant enclaves of European cities in the process, to realize that whether or not they happen to be located in traditional nation-states where political and other relations are meant to be defined in the language of citizenship, such networks and enclaves operate according to the norms of the global marketplace, which make for a whole new world of cosmopolitan relations between people. It is as if the émigré world of Joseph Conrad's novel *The Secret Agent* has suddenly ceased being a space merely of parochial cosmopolitanism to become instead its universal location.

In this sense a place like Dubai, and the Persian Gulf region as a whole, is simply a larger and more prosperous version of immigrant and student enclaves around the world, to many of which it is actually connected even if only by way of providing a major transportation hub linking Asia, Africa, Europe and the Americas. Whatever the case, the new world of social and other relations that is represented by Dubai is the same one from which the jihad is constituted. And maybe this explains why the jihad re-constitutes the Middle East or Arab world by narratives other than those of the nation or region as distinct demographic and geographical entities characterized by collective political or economic cultures.

A metaphysical war

While specialists frequently acknowledge that the jihad is global in nature, they illustrate this fact only by pointing to the dispersal of its network, causes and targets. Conceptually, however, the jihad's global character is manifested in its abandonment of the freedom struggle for the religious war. In other words it is no longer because Muslim populations in certain countries happen to be oppressed by Christian or Jewish ones that the jihad is declared, but rather because the war itself is also a metaphysical one between Christians, Muslims and Jews. Fighting over material gains and losses continues to be crucial in this narrative, but what gives these battles global meaning is nothing less than a metaphysical war.

If Al-Qaeda has subordinated the particular battles of the United States, Israel, the United Kingdom and others against Afghanistan, Iraq or even "international terror" to the larger war of the Crusader-Zionist alliance against Islam, this is not simply a sign of political exaggeration or religious prejudice. By enclosing the battle of state interests within a war of religion, the jihad is staking a claim to the definition of that world of global relations in which it operates. Indeed it is metaphysics alone that makes its violence both justifiable and even possible. The difference between a war that is global

because it is about religion and one that is so because of its geographical extent should be evident. The latter, after all, is only a
neutered form of the world war, while the former aims at the
world's conversion to an entire way of thinking and seeing.

Osama bin Laden has always rejected a definition of the jihad that
is confined even to a legitimate struggle for survival or freedom. He
has been as particular about refusing to aggregate his jihad with any
war of East against West, of the oppressed against tyranny or exploitation and the like. These and various other seductive ways by which
nationalist, fundamentalist and communist movements, especially
in Asia and Africa, have often tried to universalize their struggles
are anathema to the jihad, which is willing to acknowledge injustice
and oppression elsewhere but will not falsely identify with it. It is
because the jihad is concerned neither with the undifferentiated
unity of the world's oppressed, nor even with the particular struggles of Muslims, that it has the audacity to engage in a global war. So
in his interview with Tayseer Alouni in October 2001, Bin Laden
makes it abundantly clear that the jihad is in fact a metaphysical
struggle:

Q: "Al-Qaeda is facing now a country that leads the world militarily, politically, technologically. Surely, the al-Qaeda organization does not have the
economic means that the United States has. How can al-Qaeda defeat
America militarily?"

Bin Laden: "This battle is not between al-Qaeda and the US. This is a battle
of Muslims against the global Crusaders."[15]

While he goes on to condemn America in particular and compares
its longed-for destruction to that of the Soviet Union, this initial
statement is important because Bin Laden argues that the jihad must
not be described in the ready-made terms of political life. By
insisting upon the religious nature of the war he is doing no more

than setting the terms in which the struggle is to be seen, well beyond the everyday language of a politics predicated upon old-fashioned needs, interests and ideas. And indeed we can see that traditional politics is still unable to comprehend this new conflict, for whose definition it doesn't even have a vocabulary, relying instead on the deployment of stock terms like terrorism, or at most looking at it as some crude form of a traditional freedom struggle.

Despite all the talk of Muslim fanaticism or rage, modern politics cannot comprehend religion in any terms but its own, which is to say as a kind of emotional front for supposedly real issues like freedom or justice, wealth or power. The problem with the jihad, is that while it is by no means averse either to freedom and justice or to wealth and power, it wants them on its own terms. And rather than being specifically Islamic or even religious in the emotional sense that is favoured by politics, these terms are those characteristic of new global relations that the jihad represents more fully than any other movement. In light of this situation Al-Qaeda's very deliberate description of the jihad as a metaphysical struggle between Christianity, Judaism and Islam should be seen for what it is—an effort to define the terms of global social relations outside the language of state and citizenship.

The war of the three monotheisms goes a long way towards displacing the language of state and citizenship that marks modern politics, not only by emphasizing the strictly religious nature of the struggle, but also by reading this back to events like the Crusades. Here, for example, are some of Bin Laden's remarks on the subject:

Our goal is for our nation to unite in the face of the Christian crusade. This is the fiercest battle. Muslims have never faced anything bigger than this. Bush said it in his own words: "crusade". When Bush says that they try to cover up for him, then he says he didn't mean it. He said "crusade". Bush divided the world into two: "either with us or with terrorism." Bush is the leader; he carries the big cross and walks. I swear that everyone who follows Bush in his scheme has given up Islam and the word of the prophet. This is very clear. The prophet has said, "Believers don't follow Jews or Christians."[16]

This is a recurring war. The original crusade brought Richard [the Lionheart] from Britain, Louis from France, and Barbarus [Frederick Barbarossa] from Germany. Today the crusading countries rushed as soon as Bush raised the cross. They accepted the rule of the cross.[17]

The rhetorical sophistication with which Bin Laden links the American president's use of the word crusade to the globe's division into two enemy camps is quite remarkable, allowing him to define the war as one of religion in the most logical of ways. After all how else can the division of the globe into opposing camps be interpreted otherwise than as a metaphysical one? The war of the monotheisms, by defining all combatants as Christians, Jews or Muslims, prevents the fragmentation of its struggle into one which could exculpate certain nations or groups like pacifists, communists and the like. The religious war universalizes the jihad historically as well as geographically while asserting its metaphysical character. Given this, it is hardly surprising to find Bin Laden supporting Huntington's "clash of civilizations" theory:

Q: "What do you think of the so-called "war of civilizations"? You always keep repeating 'Crusaders' and words like that all the time. Does that mean you support the war of civilizations?"
Bin Laden: "No doubt about that: The book mentions this clearly. The Jews and the Americans made up this call for peace in the world. The peace they're calling for is a big fairy tale. They're just drugging the Muslims as they lead them to slaughter. And the slaughter is still going on. If we defend ourselves, they call us terrorists. The prophet has said, 'The end won't come before the Muslims and the Jews fight each other till the Jew hides

between a tree and a stone. Then the tree and the stone say, "Oh, you Muslim, this is a Jew hiding behind me. Come and kill him." He who claims there will be a lasting peace between us and the Jews is an infidel.' "[18]

Huntington's book, which is popular throughout the Muslim world, argues that with the end of the Cold War and the emergence of a global marketplace, politics is no longer defined only by the kind of collective needs, interests and ideas that were formerly attached to states and citizenship. Instead fragmentary issues of culture or identity have come to the fore politically both within and without nation states. Huntington then goes on to mark out the civilizations which he thinks form the bedrock of the most distinct and irreconcilable cultural traits.[19] Whatever the validity of this argument, it has the merit of trying to chart out the global nature of a political life that is no longer bound up solely with the language of state and citizenship, and this is probably why Bin Laden cites it so approvingly.

While the irreconcilable character of the monotheistic war, reminiscent of the antagonism between capitalism and communism during the Cold War, puts the jihad beyond the language of everyday politics, we should recognize that, as in the Cold War, conversion is always a possibility on either side. For the jihad, the Jews, rather than simply the Zionists or Israelis, are the most irreconcilable of enemies, even though they have proved to be more rhetorical than real antagonists in all the great battles of the holy war. Indeed despite the usual fulminations about Jews controlling the American economy or the world's media, the jihad's anti-Semitism tends not to be cast in the classical mould. In the narrative of holy war Jews are dispensed with briefly and with a few stereotypes as common in Europe or America as they are in any part of the Muslim world. There are no long accounts of a Jewish conspiracy to take over the globe. In fact for someone like Ayman al-Zawahiri the Jews are seen merely as a branch of the American or Crusader tree. In this sense the jihad is faithful to an earlier analysis, common to Asian or African nationalists as well as to European communists, of Zionism as simply a tool of European or American imperialism. Here is a typical example of such viewpoints, from the 1998 statement by the World Islamic Front for Jihad Against Jews and Christians that was signed by Bin Laden, Zawahiri, and the leaders of Muslim movements in Egypt, Pakistan and Bangladesh:

[I]f the Americans' aims behind these wars are religious and economic, the aim is also to serve the Jews' petty state and divert attention from its occupation of Jerusalem and murder of Muslims there. The best proof of this is their eagerness to destroy Iraq, the strongest neighbourly Arab state, and their endeavour to fragment all the states of the region such as Iraq, Saudi Arabia, Egypt and Sudan into paper statelets and through their disunion and weakness to guarantee Israel's survival and the continuation of the brutal crusade[r] occupation of the Peninsula.[20]

The irreconcilable nature of Jewish antagonism is important not in itself, because Jews are meant to be the inveterate enemies of all Muslims, but only with reference to Christianity. For the jihad, then, the Jews are important only because they are allied with or have managed to seduce the support of Christians. Osama bin Laden inveighs against Jews only to warn Christians not be drawn into their battles with Muslims. So in a conversation with some of his men in May of 1998 Bin Laden makes the following entirely typical statement:

The enmity between us and the Jews goes back far in time and is deeply rooted. There is no question that war between the two of us is inevitable. For this reason it is not in the interest of Western governments to expose the interests of their people to all kinds of retaliation for almost nothing.

It is hoped that people of those countries will initiate a positive move and force their governments not to act on behalf of other states and other sects.[21]

This fairly transparent attempt to play upon Christian anti-Semitism indicates that for the jihad, Muslim relations with Christians are far more ambiguous and open to negotiation than those with Jews. In fact the name Christian itself is not used to identify the enemy, but rather the word Crusader, which implies that there might exist Christians who are not Crusaders. For example in one of Ron Haviv's photographs taken in Kabul after the fall of the Taliban we see what remains of Al-Qaeda's abandoned and looted office. Lying beside a two-dollar coupon for a breast pump made by Ross are two videotapes. One is titled *Jesus* and bears an attestation of authenticity from *Time* magazine. The other is a "word-for-word" depiction of the Book of Genesis, part of a series called *The Bible on Video*.[22] Apart from defying the Taliban's ban on films, and the more general Muslim prejudice against portraying sacred figures like Jesus, to say nothing of their explicitly Christian interpretation, these videotapes suggest the important place that Christianity might occupy in the landscapes of Al-Qaeda's holy war. We have already noted the Christian origins of the Middle East as a site of monotheist conflict, to which these videotapes might well bear witness. More important, however, is the fact that the jihad has meaning only in the context of a three-way struggle between the monotheistic faiths, not simply a two-way battle between Christians and Jews on the one side and Muslims on the other. A triangular struggle in which the possibility of each party changing sides is always present. And the most appropriate of sites for this unpredictable war happens to be that area known as the Middle East or the Arab world. This is how the geographies whose control provided the bases of traditional politics have finally been dismembered and re-constituted along metaphysical lines.

A community of rivals

If on the one hand the jihad as a war between the three monotheisms assumes its universality by abandoning the old politics of state and citizenship, on the other hand it lapses into the most parochial of struggles by the same token. After all there is a complete failure even to take into account the jihad's actual frontiers in China, India and South-East Asia. Despite its alliances with local Muslim groups fighting Hindus, Buddhists or communists in Asia, a movement like Al-Qaeda has nothing to say about them. In fact whenever Osama Bin Laden has been asked about such struggles he seems either to ignore the enemy who happens not to be a monotheist, or to identify him with the Crusader-Zionist alliance. The following sentence from an interview of November 9, 2001 with Hamid Mir for the Pakistani newspapers *Dawn* and *Ausaf* suggests that America is to be attacked for all attacks against Muslims:

America and its allies are massacring us in Palestine, Chechnya, Kashmir and Iraq. The Muslims have the right to attack America in reprisal.[23]

In a videotaped conversation with some of his men in May 1998, Bin Laden even suggests that those who direct the jihad against enemies who are not monotheists ought to revise their strategy:

Q: "What is your relationship with the Islamic movements in various regions of the world like Chechnya and Kashmir and other Arab countries?"

Bin Laden: "Cooperation for the sake of truth and righteousness is demanded from Muslims. A Muslim should do his utmost to cooperate with his fellow Muslims. But Allah says of cooperation that it is not absolute for there is cooperation to do good, and there is cooperation to commit aggression and act unjustly. A Muslim is supposed to give his fellow

Muslim guidance and support. He (Allah) said 'Stand by your brother be he oppressor or oppressed.' When asked how were they to stand by him if he were the oppressor, He answered them, saying 'by giving him guidance and counsel.' It all goes to say that Muslims should cooperate with one another and should be supportive of one another, and they should promote righteousness and mercy. They should all unite in the fight against polytheism and they should pool all their resources and energy to fight the Americans and the Zionists and those with them. They should, however, avoid side fronts and rise over the small problems for these are less detrimental. Their fight should be directed against unbelief and unbelievers.'[24]

Obviously Bin Laden is not recommending that theatres of war like Chechnya and Kashmir be ignored, but saying that the enemy in any case should be the Christian or Crusader and the Jew. And while his attempts to consolidate the jihad and push it in a single direction might make strategic sense, it also indicates that he has no way of thinking about the struggle in anything but monotheistic terms— despite the condemnation of polytheists and atheists (both words which are also used to refer to enemies who claim to be Muslim). And it is this inability to think beyond monotheism that finally forces the jihad back to the Middle East and the West, at least conceptually if in no other way. Muslims have had a long acquaintance with non-Islamic Asia, and perhaps even a richer, more complex set of interactions with Zoroastrians, Buddhists and Hindus than with Christians and Jews. Since the rise to world dominance of Europe in the eighteenth century, however, the monotheistic world has remained the primary focus of Muslim thought both east and west, and in this the jihad is no exception. So in his famous declaration of war against the United States in 2001, Osama bin Laden makes it clear that the real enemies of Islam are not idolaters or polytheists but, in an extraordinary move, the so-called people of the book, monotheists with whom Muslims claim a religious kinship:

Those youths know that their rewards in fighting you, the USA, is dou-
ble than their rewards in fighting someone else not from the people of
the book.[25]

Given its global dispersal, the jihad's failure to comprehend the
world outside monotheism, understandable though this might be in
political terms, makes the monotheistic world itself into its refuge—a familiar place of retreat from Islam's frontiers with China
or India, Buddhism or Hinduism. In other words the very conflict
that the jihad sets up between the three monotheistic faiths represents its community, since these enemies are also its interlocutors.
After every battle among them, the bonds linking Christians, Muslims and Jews become stronger, because they exclude every other
enemy as well as every other interlocutor. Nowhere is this more
evident than in the anti-Soviet jihad, which laid the groundwork for
today's jihad in almost every way, though it did so in religiously and
intellectually the most impoverished of ways, without considering
communism to be any kind of global interlocutor. Insofar as they
were not considered Christians, the Soviets comprised the most
abstract of enemies, quite deprived of the elaborate monotheistic
context within which the jihad places the United States or Israel
today. At most they were linked to the Western powers by the old
narrative of imperialism.

Sometimes, indeed, the Soviets were juxtaposed with the Americans and hence it became the fashion to describe the Soviet Union
by the name Kisra (Khusro), used in the Quran of the Persian emperor, who was a Zoroastrian, while the United States was called
Qaysar (Caesar) after the Byzantine emperor, who was a Christian.
Persia and Byzantium were the two superpowers of Muhammad's
time, to whose rulers he wrote inviting them to accept Islam. If
Khomeini repeated the Prophet's action in sending a similar letter

to Gorbachev, the jihad adopts the same conceit but only in order to follow Islamic history by destroying first Kisra and then Qaysar. It is the defeat of Kisra, then, that makes the jihad's world of monotheism possible rhetorically as much as in any other way. For with the end of the Cold War, a whole way of conceiving and conducting global politics was terminated, bringing to the fore monotheism as a way not only of thinking about politics in the new world, but also as a refuge from it.

The caliphate to come

The monotheistic world, however, cannot forever be dominated by a three-way war between Christians, Jews and Muslims. It must finally be subordinated to the one authority that represents the jihad's vision of the future—the caliphate. Yet the caliphate is not a political vision so much as a metaphysical category. It remains only an ideal, with neither a description nor any concrete plan to set it up. And in fact the caliphate's role thus far is simply conceptual, allowing the jihad to abandon the political geography of the Cold War, made up of national states grouped into various alliances, for a completely de-territorialized and even anti-geographical space, since the caliphate imagined by the jihad possesses neither centre nor periphery. The favourable references of men like Osama bin Laden to the Ottoman Empire are extraordinary, for they reflect nostalgically upon Turkish suzerainty over the Arabs, who won independence from Turkey only to fall into the clutches of the European powers. After having been a dead letter for well over half a century, the caliphate has suddenly re-emerged as a living category, in no matter how metaphysical an incarnation. We might recall here that the last movement in support of the caliphate and its restoration was the mass agitation of Indian Muslims after Turkey's defeat in the First World War.

The caliphate, therefore, represents the future of the monotheist struggle in Muslim lands. This it does not in the form of a political or even geographical order but by defining Islam's future victory as a set of global relations outside the political language of state and citizenship. The mutual enmity of the three monotheistic faiths is transformed under the caliphate into a relationship of proximity rather than of distance. Defined as a set of global relations, Islam no longer remains one monotheism among others, let alone the truest of these, but the religion of their final communion, as it is meant to be the summation of both Judaism and Christianity. Osama bin Laden plays upon this long-established thesis of Islam as mono-theism's synopsis in his "Letter to America" of November, 2002, when discussing religious rights in Palestine:

It brings us both laughter and tears to see that you have not yet tired of repeating your fabricated lies that the Jews have a historical right to Pal-estine, as it was promised to them in the Torah. Anyone who disputes with them on this alleged fact is accused of anti-Semitism. This is one of the most fallacious, widely-circulated fabrications in history. The people of Palestine are pure Arabs and original Semites. It is the Muslims who are the inheritors of Moses (peace be upon him) and the inheritors of the real Torah that has not been changed. Muslims believe in all of the Prophets, including Abraham, Moses, Jesus and Muhammad, peace and blessings of Allah be upon them all. If the followers of Moses have been promised a right to Palestine in the Torah, then the Muslims are the most worthy nation of this.[26]

The caliphate's right to Palestine is premised here upon Islam's uni-versality, which, according to Bin Laden, makes Muslims not only into the heirs of Jews and Christians, but even into the truest of Jews and Christians. There is a constant mirroring of Judaism and Chris-tianity in the words and acts of the jihad, which does far more along these lines than take from its predecessors the notion of a holy land.

Is it simply a coincidence, for example, that one of Osama bin Laden's fortified camps in Afghanistan was called Masada? Usually translated from Arabic as 'the lion's lair,' Masada might refer also to the Jewish fortress of Masada that was taken by the Romans in 72 AD. The story of Masada, after all, which became one of the great founding narratives of the Israeli state, ends in the collective suicide of its Jewish warriors in the face of Rome's overwhelming might. What could be more appropriate for Al-Qaeda? By representing in itself the community of monotheists, therefore, Islam claims to be the only religion capable of bringing such communion about extraneously, under the hegemony of the caliphate. And this it can do because, as Bin Laden repeats time and again, only Muslims believe in all the monotheist prophets, drawing no distinctions among them. Islam has become the democracy of monotheism.

MEDIA AND MARTYRDOM

The jihad is defined not by its various local causes, nor even by the individual biographies of its fighters, but as a series of global effects that have assumed a universality of their own beyond such particularities. Indeed the dispersed and disparate acts of the jihad provide proof enough of this, dispensing as they do with the traditional orders and genealogies of Islamic authority, as well as with an old-fashioned politics tied to states and citizenship. Perhaps the most important way in which the jihad assumes its universality, however, is through the mass media. As a series of global effects the jihad is more a product of the media than it is of any local tradition or situation and school or lineage of Muslim authority. This is made explicit not only in the use of the mass media by the jihad, whose supporters refer to it constantly, but also in the numerous conversion stories that feature media. Here, for instance, is an account of the martyr Suraqah al-Andalusi's conversion to the jihad:

One day he came across an audio cassette called *In the Hearts of Green Birds*. After hearing this cassette, he realized that this was the path that he had been searching for, for so long. This was shortly followed by various videos showing the Mujahideen from Bosnia. To him, it was as if he had found a long lost friend, from whom he could not depart. *In the Hearts of Green Birds* deeply moved him as it narrated the true stories of men who personified

87

the message that they carried, men who were prepared to give up their most precious possession (life) in order to give victory to this Message.[1]

What is interesting about this passage is not so much Suraqah al-Andalusi's inspiration by audio and videotapes, but the fact that for him these seem to have been unrelated to any local group or particular school of thought. The future martyr's encounter with the jihad through mass media appears to have been entirely abstract and individual, allowing him to break with locally available forms of Islamic authority. This process, whether real or rhetorical, is common enough in the biographies of the jihad's supporters, for instance that of Omar Sheikh, the Anglo-Pakistani kidnapper convicted for the murder of *Wall Street Journal* reporter Daniel Pearl, who also claims to have been inspired by a documentary on the Bosnian war.

But the role of mass media in the jihad goes further than mere influence. Instead the jihad itself can be seen as an offspring of the media, composed as it is almost completely of pre-existing media themes, images and stereotypes. Like the murderous Freddy, in the Hollywood horror film *Nightmare on Elm Street*, the jihad appears simply to bring to life and make real the media's own nightmares. Slavoj Zizek, for one, has written about the strong sense of déjà vu accompanying the attacks of 9/11, which had as it were been foretold by Hollywood—to the degree that many viewers tuning in to the destruction of the World Trade Center live on television thought initially that they were watching a film.[2] No matter how temporary, this inability to distinguish between reality and fiction (both after all being available only by way of the media) is crucial to the jihad as a global movement.[3] Yosri Fouda and Nick Fielding, in their book *Masterminds of Terror*, describe how the inevitable conspiracy theories making the rounds after the attacks were often dominated by media images. In Saudi Arabia one very popular theory that sought to blame the US government for the destruction of the World Trade Center, had as its evidence the following dialogue between an FBI agent and his colleague from the Hollywood film *The Long Kiss Goodnight*:

"1993, World Trade Center bombing—remember? During the trial one of the bombers claimed that the CIA had advance knowledge. [*Laughing sarcastically*] The diplomat who issued the terrorist visa was CIA. It is not unthinkable they paved the way for bombing purely to justify a budget increase."

"You telling me you gonna fake some terrorist thing just to get some money out of the Congress?"

"Well, unfortunately, Mr. Hennessey, I have no idea how to fake killing 4,000 people. So, we're just gonna have to do it for real—umm, and blame it on the Muslims naturally."[4]

The irony of such conspiracy theories is that their deep distrust of the mass media is matched by an equally profound faith in the evidence it offers, so that supposedly factual news reports are rejected in favour of apparently fictional movies, both from the same source. And while this might well be symptomatic of our access to both fact and fiction being determined by the media, the audience's efforts to detect some truth beyond the media by spotting its supposedly accidental admissions of truth in movies like *The Long Kiss Goodnight* also betrays the fact that simple political intentions no longer suffice to explain events in a global landscape.

Rather than seeing in the conspiracy theory a desire to find, behind the world of appearances, some old-fashioned reality determined by individual and collective intentions, I see in it the recognition of a landscape of global effects in which events can no longer be attributed to simple intentions and have become almost ineffable. In such theories, after all, it is precisely a world determined by intentions that has disappeared from view, while the media narrative on offer has lost the ability to convince its audience of any other kind of intentionality.

Whether or not the jihad's acts are influenced by pre-existing media stereotypes, they invariably occur in the form of events already packaged, as it were, for media distribution. Media packaging is also common among those who might not support the jihad but have been affected by it. For example in photographs released by Reuters of women in the Pakistani city of Multan protesting the beheading of their countrymen by the Islamic Army in Iraq in July 2004. The pictures show demonstrators carrying English-language placards blaming the Pakistani government for the deaths, each of which bears the name of a Pakistani music company printed decoratively at the top. No doubt anticipating the massive exposure these signs would receive in the media, an enterprising Pakistani firm seems to have sponsored them.[5] The global exposure of these English language signs could do very little for sales of such CDs abroad, but they might well reach an English-speaking Pakistani audience in a much more effective way by taking this international route. Al-Qaeda and its imitators are not slow to reciprocate such media-savvy moves. An Iraqi tribal leader, negotiating on behalf of the Islamic Secret Army for the release of three Indian citizens taken hostage in July 2004, advised that appeals made to the abductors by Indian film stars were more likely to succeed than direct communications from the government in New Delhi. What kind of holy warriors are these who blend so effortlessly with Hindi film fans?[6]

From spectacular attacks to sundry communiqués and beheadings, the jihad's world of reference is far more connected to the dreams and nightmares of the media than it is to any traditional school of Islamic jurisprudence or political thought. Indeed the novel practice of beheading hostages, especially on film, has spread rather like a fashion promoted in the media. Ramzi Yousef and Khalid Sheikh Mohammed, Pakistanis domiciled in Kuwait who were respectively involved in the 1993 and 2001 attacks on the World Trade Center, seem to have modelled their behaviour on that of James Bond. This is how they passed the time in between carrying out a series of strikes in South-East Asia during 1994:

The conspirators were very cool. As they planned their attacks in Manila, they took plenty of time out to enjoy themselves. After bombing the PAL (Philippines Airlines) airliner they went to Puerto Galera, a beach resort south of Manila, to take a week-long scuba-diving course. One of Khalid's girlfriends later told police that he had portrayed himself as a rich Qatari businessman. One of their meetings took place in a five-star hotel in Makati, Manila's financial district. The two men also frequented night-clubs and hotel bars. On one occasion Khalid set out to impress a lady dentist by hiring a helicopter and flying it over her clinic while talking to her on the telephone.[7]

Such "Westernized" behaviour did not in the least interfere either with the religious belief of these men, or with their fervent practice of it at other times. Nor does it indicate an exceptionally schizo-phrenic attitude, since similar swings in behaviour, terrorist out-rages apart, are common enough among Muslims, as they are no doubt among others as well. Indeed such behaviour is, if anything, yet another sign of the disintegration of old-fashioned distinctions, whether religious or political, in a universe of global effects that is best represented by the mass media.

The great battles of the jihad in Afghanistan also took on the appearance of media narratives about epic wars between rival prin-ciples. The vast technological and numerical superiority of the airborne US-led troops deployed against Al-Qaeda and the Taliban then, quite inadvertently replays media set pieces about the war between robots and humans, airborne and earth-based power, that are familiar from films such as *Dune, Terminator* or *Matrix*. In such epic confrontations, naturally, it is the very peculiarity and even savagery of the holy warrior that renders him more human than the American soldier who looks and behaves like a robot. It is in fact only the individualization of the American soldier through his perversion, for example in the photographs of torture at Baghdad's Abu Ghraib prison, that makes him human—that and his death, which, like that of Arnold Schwarzenegger in *Terminator*, finally renders the robot human by making him mortal.[8]

The spectacle of martyrdom

The ruin, the cave and the battlefield as sites of holy war and martyrdom have by their very currency become the arenas of a global Islam, displacing in this respect the shrine, tomb and holy city of the past. Sarajevo, Grozny, Kabul, Baghdad, Srinagar and even New York, like the sacred sites of old, also call forth practices of pilgrimage, donation, tourism and death, but unlike these are marked neither by tradition nor commemoration. While each of these global sites calls to and even emulates the others by making possible the movement of men, money and munitions between them, none make for old-fashioned practices of visiting and recalling, perhaps because they are by nature un-historical. Their importance lying in the sheer currency or immediacy of suffering, these sites are quickly forgotten once they become safe for visiting, or rather they survive only as names in the randomly constructed genealogy of some other, more current theatre of war and martyrdom. As sites of a global Islam, in other words, former sites of the jihad like Sarajevo are separated from their own local and regional histories to become part of the history of jihad elsewhere, in places such as Kabul, Baghdad or Manhattan.

For most Muslims, as for most people, the jihad site is experienced visually, as a landscape initially made available by way of the international media and then redacted in conversation, posters, literature, art-work and the like. Existing as they do primarily and even originally by way of reports from broadcasters like the BBC, CNN and now Al-Jazeera, these sites of a global Islam have achieved the kind of universality denied even to the most spectacular of traditional practices, such as the annual pilgrimage to Mecca. Not only do landscapes of the jihad receive more airtime than any other object identified with Islam, but they also attract the world's attention in unprecedented ways precisely because they are identified with Islam. From the broadcasts of Fox TV to newspapers and websites all over the Muslim world, images of urban destruction and fighting in often harsh terrain have come to identify not only the jihad but Islam as such.

It is no exaggeration to say that only in this globally mediated landscape does Islam become universal, uniting Muslims and non-Muslims alike in a common visual practice, even in a fundamental agreement over the Islamic nature of the spectacle that brings together people of every religious and political opinion in a strange unity. Might we say that a religious universality expressed in the vision of converting the world has been displaced here by the conversion of vision itself, to make of Islam a global spectacle built out of the convergence and complicity of innumerable lines of sight? It is as the object of this seeing that Islam becomes universal, if only in the particularity of the caves, ruins and battlefields of its own martyrdom.

The jihad's battlefields become sites of a global Islam only when they are in the news, which is why combatants, funds, and supplies, not to mention the world's attention, move from one battlefield to another, because the content of the jihad is the news itself as something new. It is when they are reduced to caves and ruins that the towns and villages occupied by the jihad lose their own histories and become nothing but news, to enjoy their being in a state of immediacy. And once their particularity is destroyed, their very roots eradicated, these blasted habitations and their former occupants are transformed into universal figures. They become Muslims as such, people whose particular histories have suddenly disappeared to become part of the universal history of Islam.

Islam comes to exist universally in the places where its particularity is destroyed, the presence of its ruins on television screens bearing witness to the Muslim's universality as martyr and militant. What makes Islam universal, then, is the forging of a generic Muslim, one who loses all cultural and historical particularity by his or her destruction in an act of martyrdom.

In the paragraphs that follow, I examine how this martyrdom achieves meaning only by being witnessed in the mass media. Now witnessing itself means martyrdom, the Arabic word *shahadat* translating one term into the other, so that to have borne witness is also to be martyred. The ordinary legal term *shahadat*, to bear witness or to testify, is transformed into the word for martyrdom by fixing on the momentary act of witnessing whose subject is annihilated with the accomplishment of this testimony. There is a close link between seeing and dying in the etymology of martyrdom, just as there is in the televised image of the landscape that as news is simultaneously seen and destroyed, becoming yesterday's news at the very moment of its broadcast, because its universality depends upon its destruction.

Unlike Christian martyrdom, which also invokes the idea of witnessing, *shahadat* involves not only the person whose life is voluntarily sacrificed for the cause of God, but everyone annihilated in this cause whether willingly or not. Not only people, but animals, buildings and other inanimate objects as well may participate in the rites of martyrdom, including even those who witness the martyrdom of others without themselves being killed. After all *shahadat* is a fundamentally social and therefore inclusive act, the pity and compassion it excites among witnesses forming part of its classical as much as contemporary definition. Because martyrdom in Islam is thus connected to seeing in a much more general as well as much more specific sense than in Christianity, it is capable of cohabiting in productive ways with the global practices of news reportage. Martyrdom also includes within its ambit any number of subjects: perpetrators, victims, bystanders, other animate and inanimate witnesses, near or far, all of whom constitute by their very seeing the landscape of the jihad as a site of sociability.[9]

Only in mass media does the collective witnessing that defines martyrdom achieve its full effect, as the various attempts by would-be martyrs to film their deaths or at least to leave behind videotaped testaments, illustrates so clearly. A videotape obtained by *Time* magazine in which martyrs are shown reading their last testaments, saying goodbye to their families and blowing themselves up at various places in Iraq is the closest the jihad has yet come to creating its own form of a reality television show. The sequence of events depicted in this video is entirely scripted and replete with scenes straight from Hollywood—for instance the pose struck by one such martyr, Abu Harith al-Dosari, embracing and kissing his beloved goodbye through her veil, hardly an acceptable public spectacle for any Muslim tradition.[10] This constant reference within the jihad to mass media as the global witnesses to martyrdom sometimes

assumes the status of a mania, for example in the following passage
from an editorial in the Saudi on-line journal *Voice of Jihad* that is the
mouthpiece of Al-Qaeda in the Arabian Peninsula:

> My Muslim and *Mujahid* brothers, don't you see the Muslims being killed
> in Afghanistan and Iraq?! Don't you see, on the television screens, the
> bereaved women crying out for the Muslims' help?! Don't you see the torn
> body parts of children, and their skulls and brains scattered…?[11]

If the quotation above demonstrates anything, it is that the media's
representation of martyrdom creates a global community whose
witnessing imposes certain responsibilities upon its members. This
community, however, is not limited to Muslims, but includes all
those who bear witness. Indeed there is a sense in which even the
jihad's enemies—or victims—come to participate in the rites of
martyrdom by dying alongside its suicide bombers in spectacular
set-pieces like the attacks of 9/11. This may explain why supporters of the jihad are forever drawing parallels between its own
dead and those of its enemies, because both coalesce in a community of martyrdom made possible by the virtual intimacy of the
media, which allows each party to exchange words and deeds with
the other. Thus the following sentences from Al-Qaeda's lengthy
justification for the attacks on New York and Washington:

> It is allowed for Muslims to kill protected ones among unbelievers as an act
> of reciprocity. If the unbelievers have targeted Muslim women, children
> and elderly, it is permissible for Muslims to respond in kind and kill those
> similar to those whom the unbelievers killed.[12]

In a videotape broadcast by Al-Jazeera on October 29 2004, during
the closing phase of a bitterly contested presidential election in the
United States, Osama bin Laden repeated this justification for the
attacks of 9/11, tying it even more strongly to the viewing practices
of mass media:

God knows it did not cross our minds to attack the towers but after the situation became unbearable and we witnessed the injustice and tyranny of the American-Israeli alliance against our people in Palestine and Lebanon, I thought about it. And the events that affected me directly were that of 1982 and the events that followed—when America allowed the Israelis to invade Lebanon, helped by the US sixth fleet.

In those difficult moments many emotions came over me which are hard to describe, but which produced an overwhelming feeling to reject injustice and a strong determination to punish the unjust.

As I watched the destroyed towers in Lebanon, it occurred to me to punish the unjust the same way (and) to destroy towers in America so it could taste some of what we are tasting and to stop killing our children and women.[13]

Noteworthy is that the witnessing of which Bin Laden speaks so personally, and which affected him so deeply, was in fact a collective witnessing by way of mass media, since he never participated in the Lebanese war. It was perhaps the abstracted nature of this viewing that resulted in Bin Laden's determination to reject injustice and punish the unjust in an equally abstract manner, as a universal and so properly ethical imperative rather than a specifically political one, since what had become "unbearable" for him as a television viewer was a morally unjust situation. Yet the profound emotions that he claims were inspired by this witnessing bear little if any relation to the reality of the scene he describes. In other words while he may have reacted to images from the Israeli invasion of Lebanon in this fashion, Bin Laden's attempt to claim the destruction of tower blocks in Beirut as a precedent for those of Manhattan ignores more recent precedents, such as the attempt to destroy the World Trade Center in 1993. Moreover the proposal to fly planes into the twin towers was suggested to him by an outsider, Khalid Sheikh Moham-med. So the mediated witnessing of terror in Beirut, which Bin Laden tells us set a precedent for his equally mediated witnessing of terror in New York, together make up a media narrative in which one scene is exchanged for another, creating a community of exchanges between the jihad and its enemies.

The statements quoted above, selected from innumerable others on the reciprocity in death between Muslims and their enemies, justify such equivalence and even equality as neither necessary for winning the war nor even as a form of revenge. Instead it is reciprocity for its own sake that is ascribed value, making for the only kind of community possible between holy warriors and their antagonists, who are otherwise unequal in every respect—the community of death. And while the doctrine of reciprocity allows terrorists to avoid claiming responsibility for killing others by making such acts seem like the unintentional effects of some prior cause, killing oneself does exactly the opposite, by asserting intentionality in the most paradoxical of ways. It is as if suicide has become the only way in which responsibility, and thus also humanity, can be claimed in a universe of global effects. Here, then, is an extraordinarily clear acknowledgement, by a Hezbollah fighter in Lebanon, of the community created by way of martyrdom between enemies who in death become interchangeable precisely as human beings:

The Americans pretend not to understand the suicide bombers and consider them evil. But I am sure they do. As usual, they are hypocrites. What is so strange about saying: "I am not going to let you rob me of all my humanity and my will?" What is so strange about saying: "I'd rather kill you on my own terms and kill myself with you rather than be led to my death like a sheep on your terms?" I know that the Americans fully understand this because this is exactly what they were celebrating about the guy who downed the Philadelphia flight on September 11, the one where the hijackers failed to hit their target. Isn't that exactly what he must have said when he decided to kill himself and everyone else by bringing the plane down? Didn't he say to those hijacking him: "I'd rather kill you on my own terms and kill myself with you rather than be led to my death like a sheep on your terms?" They made a hero out of him. The only hero of September 11. They are hypocrites, the Americans. They know as much as we do that as a human being we all have the capacity to rush enthusiastically to our death if it means dying as a dignified being.[14]

The sociable nature of the jihad is evident in this passage, with martyrdom making a community possible by the collective witnessing of mass media. For it is this bearing of witness that allows Americans and the world at large to know that the martyrs of 9/11 and their victims were interchangeable and equal in death—a death that was important because it offered them both the possibility of becoming human.

Seeing is believing

Martyrdom creates a global community because it is collectively witnessed in mass media. These witnesses are therefore part of the jihad's struggle either as friends or enemies. Unlike European or American debates on this war, which focus on the lack of knowledge, agreement and so community between its combatants, the jihad assumes knowledge and therefore responsibility among all who witness its struggle. This knowledge and responsibility result from the global community that is created by the spectacle of martyrdom in mass media, which no amount of bias or propaganda can quite conceal. Ayman al-Zawahiri's description of this responsibility is entirely typical and repeatedly invoked by supporters of the jihad:

It also transpires that in playing this role, the western countries were backed by their peoples, who were free in their decision. It is true that they may be largely influenced by the media decision and distortion, but in the end they cast their votes in the elections to choose the governments that they want, pay taxes to fund their policy, and hold them accountable about how this money was spent.

Regardless of method by which these governments obtain the votes of the people, voters in the western countries ultimately cast their votes willingly. These peoples have willingly called for, supported, and backed the establishment of and survival of the State of Israel.[15]

The interesting thing about this argument, which would justify attacks against American civilians, is that it advocates the responsibilities of democracy in the most full-blooded way. It is because the United States is a functioning democracy that its citizens can be held responsible for the actions of their government, something that might not apply to people living under dictatorships. Such holding responsible of the American people to the implications of their democracy puts the jihad in the curious position of taking this democracy more seriously than Americans themselves. After all the assignation of responsibility in the jihad is itself an inclusive and even democratic act because, as we have seen, it presupposes the existence of a global community of equals.

The passage quoted above, however, also begins to consider what responsibility might look like in a universe of global effects. How can such responsibility either be claimed or assigned in a world of media distortion and political coercion, where people are often ignorant of the true nature of things, or deceived about them? How can Ayman al-Zawahiri recognize the constraints of ignorance and deception, as indeed he does, and still opt for a full-blooded version of popular responsibility? Perhaps because responsibility here does not depend on a knowledge of some truth, so that like the citizen who breaks a law without knowing it, the American who supports an anti-Muslim government without knowing it is held responsible for his actions. Rather than depending upon the knowledge of truth as an intellectual or epistemological entity, therefore, such responsibility depends upon an ethical choice made available only by the media's representation of martyrdom. In other words media images of the jihad, no matter how distorted or deceptive, force its audience of Americans and others into an ethical choice to support either its Muslim victims or their infidel oppressors—and all who make this choice are held responsible for it, having become participants in the jihad irrespective of their knowledge about its truth. The very spectacle of martyrdom imposes certain responsibilities upon its witnesses, and not the notion of some objective truth that might be found hidden behind it, as if behind a veil of appearances.

Media images of martyrdom have no epistemological status, since their truth never becomes a subject for discussion in the holy war. Indeed knowledge as an epistemological category does not exist in the jihad, which usually demonstrates its truth by pointing to the same media images that are otherwise denounced as distorted and deceptive, thus suggesting that knowledge in some objective sense is not an issue for it at all. Indeed it is remarkable how widely the jihad diverges from traditional political movements in this respect. Whether liberal or conservative, communist or fascist, these were much concerned with the illusory nature of appearances and the public ignorance—or false consciousness—that resulted from it. The rhetorical task of old-fashioned politics, then, was to distrust appearances and reveal the truth lying behind them. In the jihad, however, despite the standard accusations of media bias and distortion, as in the quotation from Zawahiri above, there exists no rhetorical anxiety about the concealment of truth, which is in fact available in its appearances as a media spectacle.

While I have linked the jihad's role as a media spectacle to Muslim notions of martyrdom, I do not wish to suggest that this role somehow derives from such notions. The community of witnesses created by the media spectacle, and its ethical responsibility for the holy war, makes sense even without the etymology of the word *shahadat*. The jihad posits the existence of a global community, one that is formed by martyrdom as a bearing of witness through mass media in order to hold people, and even the whole world, responsible in some way for its struggle. Such responsibility, therefore, depends upon the unproblematic availability of the jihad's truth in martyrdom, beyond any theory of ignorance or deception. After all truth here has become an ethical rather than epistemological fact. This does not mean that there are no attempts at media deception, only that the spectacle of martyrdom makes ignorance inexcusable, as if by the sheer excess of its violence. So apart from acknowledging the responsibility assigned them by the jihad, it is hypocrisy and not delusion that is the only other attitude expected of people. Hypocrisy, an accusation levelled in the Quran against those who claimed to be Muslim out of convenience, has become the jihad's most damning charge, referring now to the self-interested lies not only of Muslims but of all those concerned with its struggle.

Ultimately the spectacle of martyrdom is its own proof, a sacrifice whose selflessness transforms the jihad into a practice of ethics. Indeed as an ethical performance the act of martyrdom is a perfectly circular one, since it proves itself by itself without the help of any outside truth. And this is how it is invariably described in the jihad, as a leap of faith that affirms itself by itself. Thus the following poem by an Al-Qaeda member, Abu Salman al-Maghribi, on one of the suicide bombers who destroyed the American embassy in Nairobi:

Your good action caused flags to fly at half-mast, and your chaste face smashed idols.
You said goodbye to lions and their young cubs and strode through a door where you were an imam.

Finding other courses of endeavour crowded, you selected a course where there was no crowd.

With high resolve, you looked with disdain on death and defeated the massive army of infidelity and doubt.[16]

Because the act of martyrdom occurs as a media spectacle, its self-justifying character has as much to do with the nature of mass media as it does with anything Islamic. And in fact it is the media's inability to refer either to a distinct audience or indeed a distinct reality that accounts for the self-justifying character of martyrdom—because it can have no access to anything beyond itself. The media's audience, after all, is completely abstract, its existence assumed only as a set of standardized categories.[17] This means that no traditional communication is really possible within mass media, whose audiences have been transformed into mere consumers in quantitative terms.[18] The community created by the spectacle of martyrdom, therefore, is purely abstract, as much an effect of the media as the jihad itself. And in fact the abstract audience of the jihad as a media spectacle implies that it is truly witnessed only by a universal being who is everywhere and so nowhere: who else but God?

More than this, the proliferation of information and of opinions about information in mass media also renders the reality it describes unfathomable, thus giving rise to the kind of conspiracy theories or confusion between fact and fiction mentioned earlier. This is so because there can be no access to reality except through the media itself, which thus transforms reality as such into mere information, to be endlessly interpreted in opinion-making.[19] Niklas Luhmann points out the ethical rather than epistemological attitude that results from this transformation of reality into information:

We just learn to observe the observing and to experience the conflict itself as reality, since differences are to be expected. The more information, the greater the uncertainty and the greater too the temptation to assert an opinion of one's own, to identify with it and leave it at that.[20]

Luhmann also links this ethical attitude towards the media spectacle with the emergence of new religious movements, whose zeal, rather than following the old model of enthusiasm that might have implied some access to divine inspiration, actually does the opposite:

One can step up and say: this is my world, this is what we think is right. The resistance encountered in the process of doing this is, if anything, a motive for intensification; it can have a radicalizing effect without necessarily leading to doubts about reality. And unlike in the older model of 'enthusiasm,' one does not need to rely on divine inspiration nor to give oneself over to the opposite assertion that this is an illusion. It is sufficient to weld together one's own view of reality with one's own identity and assert it as a projection. Because reality is no longer subject to consensus anyway.[21]

Martyrdom as a media spectacle is therefore self-contained, foregoing any reference to an outside audience or reality without in any way questioning their existence. Indeed it is the inaccessible or better yet unfathomable nature of such entities that makes martyrdom into an ethical rather than an epistemological or political performance. As the supreme performance of the jihad, martyrdom does not depend on the knowledge either of an external audience or of an external reality, serving instead as its own proof.

The art of war

Because ignorance and therefore false consciousness do not exist in the world of the jihad, neither does the liberal effort of persuasion. Unlike political movements in the past, including fundamentalism and terrorism in the service of some national cause, the jihad's votaries do not attempt to convert people to their vision of things.

In fact such conversion, as we noticed in the first chapter, might well occur only as an accidental effect of the jihad's ethical performance. So while statements, communiqués, interviews and other forms of information and explanation emanate from the jihad, these, too, can be seen as performances of an ethical kind. This performance of the ethical is signalled by the novel way in which the jihad presents itself in mass media, as a visual presence that far exceeds any instrumental attempt either to persuade or terrorize people in the service of any cause.

On the one hand there are the extraordinary videotapes of hostages who are beheaded, often following the reading out of statements by victims and captors alike. To some extent these follow traditional terrorist practice, claiming that hostages are killed because demands have not been met by their governments, but the bloody nature of the killing is unprecedented. Often described as ritualistic (but why more so than any other form of execution?), such beheadings very deliberately depart from earlier forms of terrorist murder because, I suspect, it is the media spectacle itself rather than the death of any victim that is of primary importance for them. These beheadings, then, which themselves seem to imitate media images of Muslim barbarity, are part of this media's flirtation with representations of violence as much as they are of any peculiarly Islamic form of sacrifice. It is almost as if the jihad is here fulfilling the desire of mass media for real horror, but on the same model as reality television shows. So while this reality strives to achieve authenticity by its very extremity, just as in reality television shows, it in fact achieves exactly the opposite by becoming a piece of theatre.

On the other hand there are the videotaped interviews and conversations of key Al-Qaeda figures, which depart from traditional representations of political, military or religious leaders, including terrorists, rebel commanders and the like. Unlike old-fashioned forms of direct address, where such leaders would deliver stern statements to camera, many of the films featuring Bin Laden or Zawahiri have the character of home videos, in which the camera is never directly addressed and appears to be spying on a private gathering. Instead of issuing terse warnings, the founder of Al-Qaeda engages in long and meandering conversations that have to be picked over for newsworthy information. Indeed it is only in his interviews with broadcasters like ABC, CNN or Al-Jazeera, and not in Al-Qaeda's own recordings, that Bin Laden is portrayed addressing himself directly to the camera—the one exception so far being a videotape released by Al-Jazeera on October 29, 2004, four days before the US presidential elections, in which Bin Laden reads a statement while standing at a podium against a neutral brown background that matches the colour of his cloak. Otherwise his rambling conversations, reminiscent in many respects of Khomeini's interviews during his French exile, are clearly represented not as intelligible communications to some external audience, whether Muslim or not, but rather as private performances.

Even when Osama bin Laden directly addresses the camera this is done in the most private or domestic of ways, dispensing with the public forms of address characteristic of leaders like the late Yasser Arafat. So Bin Laden and Zawahiri have posed for the cameras of news agencies sitting or standing side by side with shy smiles on their faces, looking for all the world like two uncles in a nephew's family album. Apart from some appropriately militaristic images of Al-Qaeda camps in Afghanistan, the use of arms in representations of its leader are equally domestic in character. Osama bin Laden, rarely portrayed without his Kalashnikov, appears to treat it more as a toy than a weapon. When it is not carelessly balanced against a wall or lazily handled by its owner, the gun lies flat across his folded legs, like a baby in its father's lap. In fact it is difficult to escape the impression that the military paraphenalia present in images of Al-Qaeda are props in a performance where their usual roles have been subverted by the inexplicably private or idiosyncratic behaviour of the mujahidin. Again it was Osama bin Laden's sudden appearance during the 2004 American elections, following a prolonged silence, that broke these visual rules. In this videotape a turbaned and cloaked Bin Laden has been completely divested of military trappings and appears to be speaking in the guise of an international statesman—his statement having been shorn of both the religious references and the bloodthirsty tone that had characterized previous utterances. Indeed Bin Laden's posture, demeanour and even surroundings bear a resemblance to those of speakers addressing the U.N. General Assembly, to say nothing of the campaign addresses by either candidate for the US presidency.

I shall return to the videotape of what was effectively Osama bin Laden's campaign advertisement below. His sudden change of manner and appearance mock and caricature conventional forms of statesmanship, especially given the heavily satirical tone Bin Laden adopts. Whether or not it was intended to be satire, however, his unexpected performance made the videotape appear all the more like a piece of theatre. But then it is precisely the jihad's unwillingness to distinguish between media spectacle and political reality that most effectively illustrates its character as an ethical performance, as exemplified in a video, recorded in Afghanistan in November 2001, showing Osama bin Laden and several companions discussing the 9/11 attacks:

Sulayman [Abu Guaith]: I was sitting with the Shaykh in a room where there was a TV set. The TV broadcast the big event. The scene was showing an Egyptian family sitting in their living room, they exploded with joy. Do you know when there is a soccer game and your team wins, it was the same expression of joy. There was a subtitle that read: 'In revenge for the children of Al Aqsa, Usama Bin Ladin executes an operation against America.' So I went back to the Shaykh [*meaning UBL*] who was sitting in a room with 50 to 60 people. I tried to tell him about what I saw, but he made a gesture with his hands meaning: 'I know, I know...'[22]

This is a portion of the videotape where Bin Laden and his companions are speaking of prophetic dreams about the destruction of the World Trade Center, so it is not entirely clear whether Sulayman Abu Guaith is recounting a dream or real experience. But this uncertainty is itself full of interest because it ignores the distinction between fantasy and reality without in the least doubting either. And this deliberate ignorance is only reinforced by the fact that Abu Guaith at no point refers to anything outside the media, even deferring the reality of 9/11 in a series of media references, so that it is made available by Abu Guaith watching an Egyptian family on his television who are watching the collapse of the twin towers on their television. What is more the event itself is compared to a soccer match, which is to say a game, a televised spectacle, and not to some unmediated form of reality. As it turns out, comparing the attacks of 9/11 to televised football games, or to karate tournaments, is common in Al-Qaeda circles. This suggests that its jihad is conceived of in sporting rather than, say, apocalyptic terms, as a rule-bound contest in which the survival and indeed community of both parties is assumed. Perhaps such comparisons indicate callousness, or even a loss of touch with reality in their makers. They certainly do represent acts of the jihad as performances which are ethical because they are self-contained. Comments by Bin Laden from the same videotape provide a good example of this:

Abu-Al-Hasan Al-(Masri), who appeared on Al-Jazeera TV a couple of days ago and addressed the Americans saying: "If you are true men, come down here and face us." (…inaudible…) He told me a year ago: "I saw in a dream, we were playing a soccer game against the Americans. When our team showed up in the field, they were all pilots." He said: "So I wondered if that was a soccer game or a pilot game? Our players were pilots." He (Abu-Al-Hasan) didn't know anything about the operation until he heard it on the radio. He said the game went on and we defeated them. That was a good omen for us.[23]

The prevalence of prophetic dreams in the jihad also attests to its self-contained performance of ethics on the model of media spectacles in which all reference to external audiences and realities has been dispensed with. Yet this by no means implies the jihad's own departure from reality, only its recognition of reality's unfathomable nature. It is this that makes an act like martyrdom into something ethical, because its strictly instrumental or political aims have been overcome by the spectacle of suicide itself as a self-contained performance. And indeed given the jihad's complete lack of an old-fashioned political utopia, how else can its acts be defined except as ethical ones? The jihad's dreams, then, not only dispute all traditional distinctions between fiction and reality by their very existence, they also constitute the only kind of externality possible in the jihad as media spectacle. This sometimes leads to comic situations like the following, narrated by Osama bin Laden, in which he refers jokingly to the prevalence of prophetic dreams foretelling the destruction of the twin towers:

We were at a camp of one of the brother's guards in Qandahar. This brother belonged to the majority of the group. He came close and told me that he saw, in a dream, a tall building in America, and in the same dream he saw Mukhtar teaching them how to play karate. At that point I was worried that maybe the secret would be revealed if everyone starts seeing it in their dreams. So I closed the subject. I told him if he sees another dream, not to tell anybody, because people will be upset with him.[24]

Rather than being part of some occult tradition, the jihad's dreams and representations belong in fact to the world of mass media, whose global effects they very accurately describe. It is this world too that makes possible the jihad's acts as a set of ethical performances. Indeed all the supposedly peculiar aspects of the jihad's imagery might actually be characteristic of global movements more generally. Like these, the jihad is forced to operate in an ethical rather than political way by its inability to control or predict the future. Its actions, therefore, while being meticulously planned, do not themselves plan for any future, which thus remains open in every respect. Rather these actions occur as speculative investments in some idea of justice that cannot be anticipated, only invoked in a self-contained performance of ethics, whose effects serve merely as opportunities for further investment.

It is perhaps this freedom from a utopian politics of intentionality that gives the jihad its rich inner life. Dreams and auguries apart, the rites of martyrdom are dominated by images of freedom that appear to have nothing to do with political causality of any sort. Such, for instance, are the green birds that populate many narratives of martyrdom. We have seen from his testament that the European martyr Suraqah al-Andalusi, who was killed in Afghanistan in 2001, happened to be converted to the cause of martyrdom by an audio-cassette titled *In the Hearts of Green Birds*. The reference here is to the following tradition of Muhammad:

The Prophet (SAWS) said: "*The souls of martyrs reside in the bodies of green birds that perch on chandeliers suspended from the Throne and fly about Paradise whenever they please*." (Ahmad and At-Tirmidhi)[25]

This fanciful depiction, which is unlikely to be taken literally by any Muslim, provides the jihad with the elements of an aesthetic. It is an aesthetic that has little if any religious meaning, and is transmitted not by way of theological tracts but by the media itself—in the same way as fashions in clothing or music. These green birds are therefore aesthetic creations testifying to the rich inner life of the jihad. And it is to this inner life that I now turn.

THE DEATH OF GOD

I argued in preceding chapters that the jihad destroys traditional forms and genealogies of Islamic authority, recycling their fragments in democratic ways. Here I discuss how these fragments are recombined to produce a new kind of Muslim, whose character is revealed in his attitude towards the law. Given the jihad's dismemberment of the juridical authority that had for centuries been located in a clerical class known as the *ulama*, how is its almost obsessive concern with getting favourable rulings from this very class to be explained? To impute a juridical obsession to fighters in the holy war is no exaggeration, as Jason Burke realizes in his book *Al-Qaeda: Casting a Shadow of Terror*:

According to French intelligence, telephone monitoring of Islamic militant cells in 1999 and 2000 revealed that more calls were made about minor points of Islamic observance than the terrorist activity the cell members were supposed to be engaged in. Chechen fighters have requested fatwas on the legality of telling hostages they were to be released and then killing them, even after the actual murders.[1]

To explain such obsessive behaviour by pointing to Al-Qaeda's need for religious credibility in the Muslim world accounts neither for the jihad's damage to this credibility itself, nor for the novel fashion in which this is deployed by the holy war. Not only do supporters of the jihad routinely attack the most venerable clerics and seminaries, accusing them of being the slaves of apostate regimes, but they also issue their own legal opinions or *fatwas* without possessing either the learning or recognition to do so. And even when advocates of the jihad do receive favourable rulings from clerics, these arrive from such dispersed and disparate sources as to undo any notion of the hierarchy and jurisdiction of clerical authority.

The importance of the juridical ruling for the jihad has little if anything to do with the latter's quest for popular or religious credibility in the Muslim world. It does, however, have everything to do with the individual Muslim's assumption of religious authority by the use of classical forms like the juridical ruling, that have been separated from an institutional basis either in the clerical class or in the state. This is why legal forms seem to have achieved an importance in the jihad precisely as forms. Take, for instance, the will of Muhammad Atta, the lead 9/11 hijacker. Written in Hamburg in 1996 and dealing mainly with Atta's instructions for his funeral ceremony, including the treatment of his body, the will generated excited comment, especially concerning its misogynistic character. What seems to have escaped notice is the sheer oddity of Atta's carrying this document at all, especially in a situation where its instructions would never be followed, even if by some accident its contents were, as indeed they were, preserved. Here is how the will begins:

IN THE NAME OF GOD ALL MIGHTY

Death Certificate

This is what I want to happen after my death. I am Mohamed the son of Mohamed Elamir awad Elsayed: I believe that prophet Mohamed is God's messenger and time will come no doubt about that and God will resurrect people who are in their graves. I wanted my family and everyone who reads this will to fear the Almighty God and don't get deceived by what is in life and to fear God and to follow God and his prophets if they are real believers. In my memory, I want them to do what Ibrahim (a prophet) told his son to do, to die as a good Muslim. When I die, I want the people who will inherit my possessions to do the following:

1. The people who will prepare my body should be good Muslims because this will reminds me of God and his forgiveness.

2. The people who are preparing my body should close my eyes and pray that I will go to heaven and to get me new clothes, not the ones I died in.

3. I don't want anyone to weep and cry or to rip their clothes or slap their faces because this is an ignorant thing to do.

4. I don't want anyone to visit me who didn't get along with me while I was alive or to kiss me or say goodbye when I die.

5. I don't want a pregnant woman or a person who is not clean to come and say goodbye to me because I don't approve of it.

6. I don't want women to come to my house to apologize for my death. I am not responsible for people who will sacrifice animals in front of my lying body because this is against Islam.[2]

From its very preamble the will describes Muhammad Atta as a martyr, since he is compared by it to the son whom Abraham had to sacrifice to God. Despite this, however, the document still envisages Atta being buried in Egypt by his family, who are instructed to dispense with traditional funerary rites that the deceased considered un-Islamic, including keening, allowing women to visit his grave, commemorating his death annually, etc. While this rejection of local custom is common enough among Muslim radicals of all kinds, that Atta should also specify in his will perfectly standard practices like being buried facing Mecca and lying on his right side is again quite odd.[3] All of this obscures the will's intended readers, who are no longer Muhammad Atta's family or indeed anyone else but rather an anonymous and abstract audience. This suggests that the will is not in fact a set of instructions at all but something formulaic—a portrait of the terrorist as a good Muslim.

Whatever prompted Atta to take this impossible will on his last flight, its formal rather than instrumental nature as a legal document follows a well-established pattern in the jihad. Thus the *bayats*, or oaths of allegiance, sworn by Al-Qaeda members to Osama bin Laden are not simply voiced publicly but signed like legal contracts—and in triplicate![4] Now such oaths were traditionally verbal rather than written. Moreover their written forms could have no meaning in a clandestine movement like Al-Qaeda, where the possibility of appealing to some external authority like the state for the enforcement of these oaths did not arise. As juridical documents, therefore, such oaths of allegiance had a formal rather than legal importance.

The famous oaths of allegiance in the Muslim tradition are those that were sworn before Muhammad and the caliphs who succeeded him, though the custom has continued for saintly and royal personages across the Islamic world. Perhaps because of its exalted origins, which would make swearing allegiance to some ordinary mortal into an act of blasphemy, a number of Bin Laden's most important associates have refused to accord him this particular form of loyalty. They include Abd al-Rahim al-Nashiri, the head of Al-Qaeda's operations in the Arabian Peninsula who was responsible for the 2000 bombing of *USS Cole* in Yemen, Khalid Sheikh Mohammed, who planned the 9/11 attacks, and Hambali, a former operational leader of Jemaah Islamiah.[5] These rejections demonstrate the absence of ideology as much as of doctrinal uniformity in the jihad, while simultaneously emphasizing the properly individual character of legal forms within it.

The same individualistic treatment of juridical forms is exhibited in Ayman al-Zawahiri's many discussions of legal matters in *Knights Under the Banner of the Prophet*. For example he often expresses surprise at how the Egyptian or Pakistani authorities broke laws that he himself did not respect and would have willingly broken. His shock is not meant simply to highlight the hypocrisy of such actions for propaganda purposes, but is perfectly genuine because it is juridical form itself that has become the sign of authority for Bin Laden's lieutenant. This is how the London-based Arabic newspaper *Al-Sharq al-Awsat*, which published selections from Zawahiri's book, summarises his shock at Egypt's attempt to secure the return from Pakistan of its nationals involved in the Afghan jihad:

He says that the Egyptian Government began to pursue the Arabs, but particularly Egyptian nationals, who had stayed on in Pakistan. The situation got (to) the point where a student at Islamabad's Islamic University who was residing legally in the country was deported. Furthermore two Egyptians who had acquired Pakistani citizenship because they had married Pakistani women were arrested. The Pakistani Government's attitude of surrender got to the point where it handed over these two naturalized Pakistanis to the Egyptian Government before the Pakistani courts could finish examining their petition, with total disregard for Pakistani law and the Pakistani constitution.[6]

Such events, writes Zawahiri, led to the bombing of the Egyptian embassy in Islamabad, itself hardly an act in conformity with Pakistan's law and constitution. But then for Zawahiri the juridical issue here is a purely formal one—not the law's substantive illegitimacy but instead its inconsistent or contradictory deployment. Indeed it sometimes appears as if backers of the jihad like Ayman al-Zawahiri are not attacking the juridical order of countries such as Egypt or Pakistan, only trying to make their governments conform to this order. So lengthy passages of *Knights Under the Banner of the Prophet* express outrage at the unjust, because partial, application of Egyptian law:

Any company owner can publish a paid advertisement demanding the cancellation of a law or an administrative decision. Any actor can criticize the laws pertaining to his profession. Any writer—such as Faraj Fawdah [who was killed by Muslim fundamentalists]—can object to and ridicule the shari'ah rulings. Any journalist can lambaste the government and object to its rules, decisions, and laws. The only one who cannot do this is the mosque preacher. This is because article 201 of the penal code says: "no one in a house of worship—even if he is a man of religion and is delivering a religious sermon—can say something that opposes an administrative decision or an existing law or regulation. Anyone who does this faces imprisonment and is fined 500 pounds. If he resists, the fine and imprisonment are doubled."[7]

Further, the only people who are not allowed to form trade unions—a right that is guaranteed even to belly dancers in Egypt—are the religious preachers and scholars.[8]

Obviously a book that recommends the annihilation of regimes it calls apostate can hardly ask at the same time for a reform of their laws so as to make them more inclusive. Zawahiri is not simply asking for religious preachers and scholars in Egypt to be given the same rights of unionization as other occupations. His concern with juridical categories is formal, with the law representing authority as such. While the substance of the law, therefore, might or might not be offensive, it is the individual's relationship with it that is crucial. In this scheme of things to follow a good law hypocritically is as good or as bad as following a bad law honestly. This is why Zawahiri, while condemning the military court under which he and many others were tried in the Sadat assassination case, still praises its president, Abd al-Ghaffar, for verdicts that he thinks were fair to the Muslim radicals declared guilty at this trial.[9] For Abd al-Ghaffar followed the law's injunctions of fairness scrupulously.

Whether religious or profane, the law and juridical categories in general assume an ethical rather than political meaning in the jihad. Representing authority as an abstract idea, judicial rulings are significant not in their own right so much as in the way people approach them. Given the important role played by hypocrisy (*munafaqat*) in the rhetorical arsenal of the jihad, it is not surprising that a hypocritical approach to authority should pose the biggest problem for what we might call its legal theory. After all an inconsistent, contradictory or self-interested relationship to the law, whether or not this is itself just, dissociates individual action from all authority and makes it arbitrary. Juridical categories, in other words, have become so fragmented and divorced from old-fashioned political or legal systems that they now function simply as personal representations of authority. It is as if Immanuel Kant's celebrated injunction to internalize the law has finally come true in the jihad, which only goes a step further by abolishing the law's externality. So the acts of the jihad, particularly martyrdom operations and the targeting of civilians, claim legitimacy by referring to legal rulings that have been disaggregated from traditional juridical systems to become ethical in a thoroughly individual sense.

Doubt and decision

In *Fear and Trembling* Søren Kierkegaard describes Abraham's sacrifice of his son Isaac (or Ishmael in the Muslim tradition) as an ethical suspension of ethics. By this he means that since Abraham had no precedent for such a sacrifice, and since God's command to him was not only incommunicable to others but went against God's own law, he could invoke nothing outside himself to justify his son's murder. Kierkegaard saw in the terrifying loneliness of Abraham's choice to obey a voice that offered no proof even of its own divinity the truth of all ethical action. After all, the kind of choice that can refer to scripture and be sure of public under-standing is no choice at all because it abdicates all responsibility for its acts. It is only a choice made without authority that can be called ethical because it takes full responsibility for its acts. The ethical suspension of ethics is in fact the suspension of those needs, inter-ests and ideas that I have placed within the realm of the political.

Practices of the jihad are ethical because they are linked neither to projects of liberation, nor to religious texts or norms in any coherent way. In fact the jihad lacks any traditional notion of religious observance or authority, something that the old clerical class and fundamentalists routinely point out, but only to draw the conclusion that the practitioners of holy war are not true Muslims. To say that the jihad's martyr, like Kierkegaard's patriarch, is given to acts other than the political, is not to claim that he has no idea of a political order or even that he despises such a thing. My point is a logical rather than a psychological one: that whatever idea of order the prophet or the martyr might otherwise entertain (and we know that Kierkegaard's Abraham by no means rejected God's law when he chose to flout it), his practice of sacrifice is an ethical act because it is not instrumentally connected to this idea of order.

Unlike both the traditional *ulama* and the fundamentalists, prac-titioners of holy war do not refer to Islamic texts in any extended or exegetical sense, and nor do they try to draw their practices from these systematically. Practices drawn from needs, interests or ideas are all instrumental because they refer outside themselves to some external authority, some project of order or liberation, which they are meant to advance. Not being political, practices of the jihad are both ethical, because complete in themselves, and material, because they do not represent anything beyond themselves. For soldiers in the jihad Islam is as fragmented an entity as any of the persons and buildings they destroy, as much a martyr as any of them, which is why it becomes available only in fragments: holy war, martyrdom, prayer perhaps, certain dietary prescriptions. Islam in this sense is not a set of ideas so much as a set of practices. As such a practice, martyrdom neither represents an idea nor is it in any way instrumental, but constitutes rather the moment of absolute humanity, responsibility and freedom as a self-contained act shorn of all teleology.

Even the paradise supposedly attained by the martyr becomes attenuated in the language of the jihad, existing almost as a rhetorical device so as not to detract from the ethical import of the act itself. And the same is surely true of Abraham's sacrifice as well, which according to Kierkegaard was also a practice distant from every idea, including that of paradise. In fact the jihad does for its warrior what Kierkegaard did for Abraham: it makes him into a Protestant, so that the Islam of the suicide bomber is an absolutely personal quality, as distant from the group identity of the traditional cleric as it is from the state ideology of the fundamentalist. Martyrdom, then, might well constitute the purest and therefore the most ethical of acts, because in destroying himself its soldier becomes fully human by assuming complete responsibility for his fate beyond the reach of any need, interest or idea. As such martyrdom constitutes an act of inauguration rather than one of retaliation. This is another way of saying that in martyrdom the Muslim becomes an individual.

Unlike the Christian tradition from which Kierkegaard draws his interpretation of Abraham's sacrifice, the Muslim tradition that is mobilized in the jihad stresses the role of Isaac/Ishmael over that of his father. Instead of dwelling upon the dilemma faced by Abraham when commanded by an unknown authority to sacrifice his son, this Muslim version of the narrative concentrates on Ishmael's willingness to be slaughtered by his father. Departing from the Jewish sources in which Isaac goes uncomprehending to his sacrifice, the Islamic story has Ishmael going eagerly to meet his maker, far more devout in this respect than Abraham himself, who continues to be a picture of anguish. This is why Ishmael is the perfect martyr, so perfect that his act of martyrdom is not sullied by the presence of an enemy, being completely self-possessed. Indeed Ishmael's devotion is more perfect than that of Abraham not because he is willing to die, but because he is even further removed from the divine command than is his father. Abraham, in other words, at least had some access to a dream and a voice that were possibly divine and thus inspiring of obedience, but Ishmael obeyed only his father. Far more than Abraham, therefore, it is Ishmael who is the true hero of Kierkegaard's book, for Ishmael obeys not God but what might appear to be his father's madness. And in this respect, too, he differs from Abraham, who famously disobeyed his own idolatrous father to follow God's command.

Now Ishmael is considered the ancestor of the Arabs, and the story of his arrival in Mecca is commemorated annually in the rituals of pilgrimage there. Moreover Ishmael's sacrifice provides the occasion for Islam's greatest festival, in which an animal is slaughtered in his place—the very substitution by which God finally saved Abraham from infanticide. And in the Muslim tradition the place of this sacrifice is that rock on Jerusalem's Temple Mount for which the Dome of the Rock is named. It is entirely fitting, therefore, that Ishmael should be a model of martyrdom for the jihad, perhaps the only such model taken from the *Quran*. Yet ultimately Ishmael was not martyred, so how does he serve as a model of martyrdom? According to some Christian as well as Muslim accounts, because his martyrdom was only postponed, and satisfied in the fullness of time with those of Jesus or of the Shiite imam Husayn. But this suggests that Ishmael's martyrdom might also be fulfilled elsewhere and even repeatedly, each new martyr executing in his own way the covenant with God that was established by Abraham's original sacrifice. Muhammad Atta, for instance, mentions Abraham's sacrifice of Ishmael in the preamble to his will, where he asks his family to treat him, retrospectively, as Abraham treated Ishmael, by asking him to die a good Muslim at God's command.[10]

Ishmael's importance as a model, I contend, is based on the fact that he goes to his death in a state of absolute uncertainty, obeying out of trust rather than evidence the equally uncertain command given to his father. It is therefore Ishmael's willingness to die in the absence rather than presence of God's command that demonstrates the latter's existence. It is the silence and even the death of God that makes religion possible in acts of faith like martyrdom. This, I suggest, is exactly the way in which the jihad deploys its practices, as personal choices that exercise individuality by sacrificing it. Perhaps it is only in this paradoxical way that the wilful individual of classical political thought is able to exist in the jihad's universe of unintended global effects. In any case the jihad's acts of faith are lent authority by juridical forms individually chosen and separated from all traditional structures of law. The fact that Ishmael comes to be the model for such a choice, not only points to the cloistered world of monotheism in which the jihad operates, but it also shows up the absence of other models that were formerly available to Sunni Islam, such as the martyrdom of those members of Muhammad's family who are especially revered by the Shia.

The death of God, I have said, marks the beginning of religion. This is particularly true of the jihad, which, in a departure from earlier examples of holy war, appears to lack any special access to divine guidance. Such direction was once provided by saintly or messianic figures like the various *mahdis* who populate Islamic history. The jihad is remarkable in that it seems to lack even the notion of a messiah or an apocalypse—though it is by no means lacking in some apocalyptic imagery—being quite unlike radical movements among Christians and Jews in this respect. Yet it is the jihad's prosaic nature that allows it to manifest the most extreme forms of faith, because these are radical only in their uncertainty and serve as their own proof. As the beginning of religion, the phenomenon that I am calling, after Friedrich Nietzche, the death of God, has by no means gone unnoticed in the Muslim world. The Indian poet and philosopher Muhammad Iqbal, perhaps the most important thinker of modern Islam, and one whose work remains hugely popular in many parts of the world, wove a whole theory of religious modernity from this one fact alone.[11]

Like many Muslim thinkers during the nineteenth and twentieth centuries, Iqbal claimed modernity to be Islam's birthright, a claim greeted with scepticism on the part of the European colonial powers who ruled much of the Muslim world. Iqbal was highly critical of the raptures and mysteries of mystical and other traditional forms of Islam that he thought had robbed it of reason and power by deflecting the attention of thoughtful Muslims from worldly affairs and leaving these in the hands of mediocrities. In rejecting, therefore, all direct, continuing or miraculous access to

divine authority, Iqbal threw Islam back upon itself, or rather upon
its own historical body, making it both modern and democratic in
the same move. Thus for Iqbal the Prophet Muhammad was the first
modern man because, in proposing that the history of prophethood
had come to a close with himself, he cut humanity off from continuing divine guidance in the form of prophecy. The advent of the
last prophet, therefore, completed the history of human freedom
that had begun with Adam's expulsion from paradise, in which
Iqbal saw the first stirrings of human freedom. In effect the modernity of Iqbal's Islam was premised upon the death of God as an actor
in the public life of Islam.

Muhammad Iqbal was only one of many Muslim thinkers who
founded the modernity of Islam on the same basis—the death of
God. While I am not concerned here with illustrating their philosophy in any detail, Iqbal himself was fully conscious of the implications of his theory, for he makes radical uncertainty the very
foundation of the Muslim's faith, which thus proves itself by its own
actions. There is no comfort of assured knowledge in Iqbal, only
ceaseless striving and passion. And it is this striving and passion in
the shadow of God's death that I contend marks the jihad with the
sign of Islam's modernity. It is as if the austere and puritanical form
of Islam that was characteristic of fundamentalism has in the jihad
suddenly blossomed forth in the full splendour of its spiritual life, as
the pinnacle of a religious modernity made possible by doubt rather
than certainty. This lesson, that the death of God is necessary for
religion's modernity, has been learnt in movement after Islamic
movement. Thus even Khomeini, who one might think would be
wedded to notions of divine presence and continuity by the Shiite
doctrine of the ever-present Imam, does the very reverse in his last
testament, where he praises the Iranian people who brought about

the Islamic Revolution as superior to those Muslims who fought for Muhammad or his successor Ali. After all, the Iranian people had achieved freedom in the absence of any access to divine authority, and were therefore far more faithful to their religion than the great and saintly personages of Islam's past.[12]

Politics into ethics

The jihad's ethics are embodied in the practice of Islam as an individual duty lacking the sanction of divine authority. Thus the jihad is authorized by the very extremity of its acts, which serve also to prove the existence of the divine being. Nothing illustrates the jihad's ethical nature so much as its aims. These are distanced from geo-political ones because metaphysical aims, as we saw in a previous chapter, are the only global ones. For in a period of globalization any attention to geo-politics alone is doomed to incompletion at best and failure at worst. After all an event occurring at the other end of the world, within a completely different geo-political constellation, might well transform one's own geography and politics quite unintentionally. Surely this is what recent events, like the global repercussions of the 9/11 attacks, so well illustrate. Thus in Al-Qaeda's so-called justification of their actions on that day, we are told very clearly that these had nothing to do with geo-political aims:

(T)he only motive of these young men was to defend the religion of Allah, their dignity, and their honor. It was not done as a service to humanity or as an attempt to side with Eastern ideologies opposed to the West. Rather it was a service to Islam in defense of its people, a pure act of their will, done submissively, not grudgingly.[13]

I shall return to the themes of dignity and honour, which feature prominently in this quotation, below. Here I want to emphasize that without in the least ignoring political matters, the jihad translates them into metaphysical and therefore global issues. Thus its invocation of the caliphate, defunct for some eighty years now, as the only order to whose establishment the struggle is dedicated. And should anyone miss the metaphysical rather than geo-political character of this order, supporters of the jihad are not averse to throwing in formerly Islamic lands like Spain and Southern Europe to round off the contours of the caliphate, rendering its strictly geo-political aims absurd. As we have already noticed, the same shift from geo-politics to metaphysics characterizes the jihad's description of the Arabian Peninsula as the land of the two holy sanctuaries.

The transformation of geo-politics into metaphysics is what makes the practices of holy war ethical, because they are thrown back on themselves to such a degree that the "final instructions" to the hijackers of 9/11 do not so much as mention any goal that they were about to die for. The instructions instead focus on the act of hijacking itself, which is transformed into a religiously significant event by its division into several steps, to each of which is attached particular prayers that the hijackers are asked to repeat, and particular rites that they are asked to perform. These latter include the shaving of body hair, the wearing of perfume and the blessing of personal objects. Also included are a line of poetry and speculations on the mystical values of Arabic letters without dots. All these things are in fact characteristic of Sufi guides to the mystical path, rather than being instructions of any sort.[14] Here is a selection:

When you ride the (T) [probably for tayyara, aeroplane in Arabic], before your foot steps in it, and before you enter it, you make a prayer and supplications. Remember that this is a battle for the sake of God. As the prophet, peace be upon him, said, "An action for the sake of God is better than all of what is in this world." When you step inside the (T), and sit in your seat, begin with the known supplications that we have mentioned before. Be busy with the constant remembrance of God. God said: "Oh ye faithful, when you find the enemy be steadfast, and remember God constantly so that you may be successful." When the (T) moves, even slightly, toward (Q) [unknown reference], say the supplication of travel. Because you are travelling to Almighty God, so be attentive on this trip.

Then [unclear] it takes off. This is the moment that both groups come together. So remember God, as He said in His book: "Oh Lord, pour your patience upon us and make our feet steadfast and give us victory over the infidels." And His prophet said: "Oh Lord, You have revealed the book, You move the clouds, You gave us victory over the enemy, conquer them and give us victory over them." Give us victory and make the ground shake under their feet. Pray for yourself and all your brothers that they may be victorious and hit their targets and ask God to grant you martyrdom facing the enemy, not running away from it, and for Him to grant you patience and the feeling that anything that happens to you is for Him. Then every one of you should prepare to carry out his role in a way that would satisfy God. You should clench your teeth, as the pious early generations did.

When the confrontation begins, strike like champions who do not want to go back to this world. Shout, "Allahu Akbar," because this strikes fear in the hearts of the non-believers. God said: "Strike above the neck, and strike at all of their extremities." Know that the gardens of paradise are waiting for you in all their beauty, and the women of paradise are waiting, calling out, "Come hither, friend of God". They have dressed in their most beautiful clothing.

If God decrees that any of you are to slaughter, dedicate the slaughter to your fathers and [unclear], because you have obligations toward them. Do not disagree, and obey. If you slaughter, do not cause the discomfort of those you are killing, because this is one of the practices of the prophet, peace be upon him. On one condition: that you do not become distracted by [unclear] and neglect what is greater, paying attention to the enemy. That would be treason, and would do more damage than good. If this happens, the deed at hand is more important than doing that, because the deed is an obligation, and [the other thing] is optional. And an obligation has priority over an option.

Do not seek revenge for yourself. Strike for God's sake. One time Ali bin Abi Talib [a companion and close relative of the prophet Muhammad], fought with a non-believer. The non-believer spat on Ali, may God bless him. Ali [unclear] his sword, but did not strike him. When the battle was over, the companions of the prophet asked him why he had not smitten the non-believer. He said, "After he spat at me, I was afraid I would be striking him in revenge for myself, so I lifted my sword." After he renewed his intentions, he went back and killed the man. This means that before you do anything, make sure your soul is prepared to do everything for God only.[15]

This last point makes the jihad's ethical enterprise clear by emphasizing the disinterested nature of its killing, which must not be carried out from any personal feeling of hatred but out of duty alone. If the aims of the jihad are difficult to reconcile with traditional geo-political concerns, its self-proclaimed grievances are even more peculiar. While in the singular each of these, such as American domination of Arab economies through corrupt client regimes, is real enough as a motive for holy war, together they form a stereotyped litany of global wrongs that add up to a list of general ethical faults, not particular political ones. Here, for instance, are some of these wrongs as detailed in Osama bin Laden's "Letter to America" of November 2002:

You are a nation that exploits women like consumer products or advertising tools calling upon customers to purchase them. You use women to serve passengers, visitors, and strangers to increase your profit margins. You then rant that you support the liberation of women.[16]

You are a nation that practices the trade of sex in all its forms, directly and indirectly. Giant corporations and establishments are established on this, under the name of art, entertainment, tourism and freedom, and other deceptive names you attribute to it.[17]

You have destroyed nature with your industrial waste and gases more than any other nation in history. Despite this, you refuse to sign the Kyoto agreement so that you can secure the profit of your greedy companies and industries.[18]

That which you are singled out for in the history of mankind, is that you have used your force to destroy mankind more than any other nation in history; not to defend principles and values, but to hasten to secure your interests and profits. You who dropped a nuclear bomb on Japan, even though Japan was ready to negotiate an end to the war. How many acts of oppression, tyranny and injustice you carried out, O callers to freedom?[19]

The freedom and democracy that you call to is for yourselves and for [the] white race only; as for the rest of the world, you impose upon them your monstrous, destructive policies and Governments, which you call the "American friends."[20]

You have claimed to be the vanguards of Human Rights, and your ministry of foreign affairs issues annual reports containing statistics of those countries that violate any Human Rights. However, all these things vanished when the Mujahideen hit you, and you then implemented the methods of the same documented governments that you used to curse. In America, you captured thousands of Muslims and Arabs, took them into custody with neither reason, court trial, nor even disclosing their names.[21]

What happens in Guantanamo is a historical embarrassment to America and its values, and it screams into your faces—you hypocrites, "what is the value of your signature on any agreement or treaty?"[22]

I have quoted his letter at such length to highlight the sheer range that Bin Laden's accusations encompass, in the process transforming them into a stereotyped litany of global wrongs more ethical than political in nature. His full list includes the following accusations against America: attacks on Muslims, support of dictatorial client regimes, theft of wealth and natural resources which are bought at negligible prices, occupation and corruption of Muslim lands, spread of immorality and debauchery in the forms of sex, usury and intoxicants, exploitation of women, environmental degradation, racism, deploying weapons of mass destruction, war crimes and violations of human rights. The fact that many of these accusations are shared with other global movements might lead one to think that they have been listed primarily for propaganda reasons, but whether or not this is the case, they certainly shift the motives for holy war beyond geo-political particularities onto a global plane. It is on this level, then, that the jihad joins movements like environmentalism or anti-globalization, not to mention those dedicated to animal rights or anti-abortion, at the forefront of ethical life today.

A rain of bullets

The ethical nature of the jihad as a global movement by no means interferes with its recognition of geo-political actualities. The long list of American wrongs in Bin Laden's letter offers a well-reasoned analysis of politics as it is conducted by the United States. But it responds to this analysis in a fashion that can only be described as ethical, perhaps because a political response is just not possible. So in *Knights Under the Banner of the Prophet* Ayman al-Zawahiri places the American-led war against Afghanistan in a geo-political context that both pre-dates Al-Qaeda and exists much beyond its control:

If the Chechens and other Caucasus mujahidin reach the shores of the oil-rich Caspian Sea, the only thing that will separate them from Afghanistan will be the neutral state of Turkmenistan. This will form a mujahid Islamic belt to the south of Russia that will be connected in the east to Pakistan, which is brimming with mujahidin movements in Kashmir. The belt will be linked to the south with Iran and Turkey that are sympathetic to the Muslims of Central Asia. This will break the cordon that is struck around the Muslim Caucasus and allow it to communicate with the Islamic world in general, but particularly with the mujahidin movement.

Furthermore the liberation of the Muslim Caucasus will lead to the fragmentation of the Russian Federation and will help escalate the jihad movements that already exist in the republics of Uzbekistan and Tajikistan, whose governments get Russian backing against those jihad movements.

The fragmentation of the Russian Federation on the rock of the fundamentalist movement and at the hands of the Muslims of the Caucasus and Central Asia will topple a basic ally of the United States in its battle against the Islamic jihadist reawakening.

For this reason the United States chose to begin by crushing the Chechens by providing Western financing for the Russian Army so that when this brutal campaign against the Chechen mujahidin is completed, the campaign can move southwards to Afghanistan either by the action of former Soviet republics that are US agents or with the participation of US troops under the guise of combating terrorism, drug trafficking, and the claims about liberating that region's women. [23]

This long-term analysis, as worthy of the State Department as it is of any self-respecting conspiracy theory, illustrates some of my principal arguments. Chief among these are the jihad's adoption of a global history by way of the Cold War, its location outside the bounds of the Middle East, its subordination of local struggles to the larger conflict of monotheism, and so forth.

The strictly political concerns of Zawahiri's analysis have to do with the alleged American desire and strategy to control the oil and natural gas of the Caucasus and Central Asia, which makes Muslims, and especially the supporters of holy war, into inveterate enemies of the United States. Given this explanation, Ayman al-Zawahiri could dispense with the language of Islam and even of jihad in order to gain allies among non-Muslims and wage a purely political war. The fact that he does not has little to do with his desire to play upon religious emotions or anything of the sort. It does however have a lot to do with the ethical nature of global movements like the jihad, which have been unable to prevail politically. Islam, therefore, is not merely a front for this struggle, but its very essence as an ethical movement—indeed it may well be politics that is the front here. Has the jihad hit upon ethics as the only way of dealing with a politically impossible situation? Osama bin Laden as Mahatma Gandhi?

My comparison of Bin Laden and Gandhi, while grotesque, is not made entirely in jest, since I think that the ethical element in holy war may very easily transform it into a non-violent enterprise. Violence, therefore, may be a necessarily short-term aspect of the new Islam that is today best represented in the jihad. Among the long-term features of this new Islam are its fragmentation, democratization and individualism, all of which I have discussed in this essay as being the very things that the jihad shares with other global movements, many of which are also to be defined only in ethical terms. Like the jihad, these movements illustrate the limitations of traditional politics everywhere, and especially in the universe of global effects that is their home. Must I describe the movements dedicated to environmentalism or anti-globalization, and contrast these with declining voter turnouts or the failure of classical notions of citizenship around the world, in order to make this point? Violence, then, might demonstrate not the jihad's politics so much as the fragmentation and transformation of politics itself as a category within it. In any holy war, after all, politics is by definition transformed into ethics.

The most telling thing about the jihad as an ethical movement is the fact that its rhetoric downplays if it does not altogether decimate a political vocabulary that includes words like liberation and self-determination, not because these are seen as unimportant, but because more important still are words like manners, civility, honour and dignity. These soft words of ethical life have become the slogans of the jihad, making it in this sense quite like those movements in the civilian life of Europe and America that also stress the positive need for respect and recognition, rather than simply the negative virtue of justice as restitution—multiculturalism for instance. The fact that shame should be a more dire predicament for the jihad than oppression, not only betrays its ethical individualism, but also demonstrates how far the holy war has drifted from the geo-politics that dominated collective violence till the end of the Cold War. So for Osama bin Laden such violence is meant not merely to defend Muslims or retaliate against their enemies, but to regain self-respect, as he makes clear in the famous declaration of war against the Americans in 2001:

The walls of oppression and humiliation cannot be demolished except in a rain of bullets.[24]

Without shedding blood no degradation and branding can be removed from the forehead.[25]

Humiliation and degradation are not elements in any *realpolitik*, they suggest instead its opposite: the reduction of a politics of needs, interests and ideas to the world of moral sentiments. Whatever the role of these needs, interests and ideas in global movements like the jihad, therefore, they have no place in it without the sentiment of hurt as an intensely personal factor. Whether these delicate moral sentiments are genuine or not, felt by those directly oppressed or only by their sympathizers, is entirely irrelevant to their rhetorical novelty and importance. We have already encountered this sentimental language of hurt and injury among the Sunni militants of Pakistan, and noted its democratic quest for recognition and even love.

It was in 1989, however, that the sentimental narrative of Muslim radicalism first achieved notoriety with the Rushdie Affair. Here it was not the theological matter of *The Satanic Verses*, nor the strictly religious issue of blasphemy against the Prophet that fuelled the outrage of Muslims worldwide, but the injury to their feelings prompted by insulting references to Muhammad in Salman Rushdie's novel. And the Prophet thus insulted was not the recipient of divine revelation, since Rushdie's speculations on the authenticity of the *Quran* and the veracity of Muhammad never became live issues during the affair. It was rather his portrayal of the Prophet as husband and statesman that exercised Muslim protesters, for whom the secular category of libel and the religious one of blasphemy seem to have become confused. The Muhammad who was insulted was not an old-fashioned religious personage so much as a model for the private and public life of Muslims, the model, in other words, of their ethical life as much as of their lives as citizens. It is in such ways as these that religion is democratized.[26]

6

NEW WORLD ORDER

During the Cold War, we are told frequently, the globe was dominated by two great powers which apportioned it between themselves by each taking a hemisphere. The United States and the Soviet Union, along with their closest allies, refrained from warring with each other because they all subscribed to the doctrine of nuclear deterrence. Countries less fortunately situated, in Africa and Asia for the most part, became the sites for their innumerable proxy wars.[1]

With the end of the Cold War, the victorious West ceased to be a merely hemispherical entity and departed from its geographical moorings. Having achieved something close to world hegemony, the West has also become a global rather than a territorial entity, hence it is now a metaphysical rather than a geographical category. Whatever elements of culture or civilization have been salvaged from the history of Europe and America to give flesh to this new metaphysical category called the West, its constantly shifting arena of operations, which can now roam over the entire globe, has dispersed its territorial base.

Having finally become universal as a metaphysical category, the West, whether defined as democracy, capitalism or anything else, has split down its geographical middle. Today's continental drift between Europe and America has nothing to do with disagreements of a political or economic nature between the new world and the old, but with the gradual fragmentation of the racial, cultural and historical affinities between them. In the last Gulf War, for example, the sharp differences that emerged between the United States and Britain on the one hand, and France and Germany (to say nothing of Russia, one of the West's newer members) on the other, indicated the dissolution of the Cold War's hemispheric politics—something that the expansion of both NATO and the European Union demonstrates institutionally.

European complaints of British and American unilateralism during the recent war in Iraq, then, accurate though they may well be, actually point to a new American even-handedness in its global policy, for which its racial, cultural and historical relations with Europe no longer form the basis of a political alliance. And indeed how could they given the vast global coalitions that the United States has had to build in both the Gulf Wars? So the Bush administration's extraordinarily harsh treatment of France in particular was meant to make it into an example for Europe as a whole. France, after all, was taunted precisely for being part of an "old Europe" whose greatness lay in the past, compared with the future greatness of countries such as Iraq and Iran, to say nothing of China and India. As Etienne Balibar puts it, Europe's role in the new global dispensation might best be described not as a constituent part of some Western alliance, but instead as a "vanishing mediator" between various global forces, racial, religious or political.[2]

America's own role as the Cold War's remaining superpower is even more precarious than that of Europe. For it is in fact America's very role as a superpower that makes it a political dinosaur, outmoded both because the enemy it was made to fight no longer exists, and because global politics is no longer defined in hemispheric or even properly geographical terms. Thus the vast coalitions that the United States forged in both Gulf Wars made the very idea of a war between territorial powers nonsensical. It also rendered the enemy that America was made to fight with its vast arsenal into an impossible abstraction. As Jean Baudrillard claims in his book on the first Gulf War, the United States can now only operate *under* its military capacity, the mutual deterrence its weaponry was meant to achieve during the Cold War having been transformed into the paralysis of self-deterrence. Confined to so-called conventional warfare, and unable even to deploy the threat of atomic annihilation, America can no longer fight wars, only conduct police operations.[3] Even if its new concerns about weapons of mass destruction falling into the hands of non-state actors do allow the United States to reinvent the concept of a global war, the all too literal disappearance of such geographically and institutionally dispersed enemies erases the target of this war as well.

The jihad, like other global movements after the Cold War, is non-geographical in nature, using the most disparate territories as temporary bases for its action. This makes it into an impossible enemy for the United States, because it exists beyond America's war-making potential. It is not an external or territorial foe to be dealt with by military action but rather the object of police action and internal security. Indeed Jacques Derrida points out that the jihad is a problem internal to the United States in every sense: not only does it necessarily work inside the West (or democracy, or capitalism) as a new global category, it does so with the geographical, financial and technological mobility that defines globalization itself. More than this, attacks like those of 9/11 were launched from within the United States by enemies who had trained there using the signs and instruments of its own power, such as civilian aircraft, to destroy similar signs like the twin towers of the World Trade Center.[4]

The jihad, suggests Derrida, demonstrates more clearly than any other movement the strictly internal character of global conflict in the wake of the Cold War. So America can only address the threat of holy war by attacking itself—subverting the constitutional provisions of its own civil liberties and impeding the demographic, financial and technological mobility that provide the foundations of its own economic might.[5] In doing so America paradoxically takes on the role of its erstwhile foe, the Soviet Union, as if in an act of mourning for the passing of the Cold War. The United States, then, becomes a suicide state, its martyrdom mirroring the many martyrdoms of the jihad. This is a point that Osama bin Laden himself makes very emphatically in his interview with CNN of October 2001. In it he claims that the attacks of 9/11 themselves were of little account in the damage they inflicted on America compared with what America will do to itself, in the process destroying the very essence of the West as a metaphysical entity:

The events of Tuesday, September 11, in New York and Washington are great on all levels. Their repercussions are not over. Although the collapse of the twin towers is huge, but the events that followed, and I'm not just talking about the economic repercussions, those are continuing, the events that followed are dangerous and more enormous than the collapse of the towers.

The values of this Western civilization under the leadership of America have been destroyed. Those awesome symbolic towers that speak of liberty, human rights and humanity have been destroyed. They have gone up in smoke. [...] I tell you freedom and human rights in America are doomed.[6]

Votaries of the jihad are well aware of the fact that their war is, properly speaking, internal to the West as a metaphysical category, and to the United States as its most formidable manifestation. Their struggle, after all, has never been directed simply by the aim to protect Muslims and their lands from attack, but instead to invite such attacks in order to draw America into a war it cannot control and must eventually lose. But this can only be accomplished by the immediate martyrdom of Muslims and the devastation of their lands, both being brought increasingly within the purview of the West as a global entity. And while this might be a price worth paying given the stakes involved, the ethics of such a martyrdom, which would destroy the enemy by destroying the self, renders any war against an external foe impossible. The interiority of the jihad to America's new world order, therefore, makes for a perverse community between these rivals.

Intimate enemies and sociable wars

Instead of addressing the West as something completely foreign, in the same way that it is itself addressed by this West, the jihad posits relations of equivalence between the two enemies. At the most basic level this equivalence is one of retaliation, something Osama bin Laden is very clear about in his Letter to America of November 2002:

Allah, the Almighty, legislated the permission and option to take revenge. Thus, if we are attacked, then we have the right to attack back. Whoever has destroyed our villages and towns, then we have the right to destroy their villages and towns. Whoever has stolen our wealth, then we have the right to destroy their economy. And whoever has killed our civilians, then we have the right to kill theirs.[7]

While the desire for proportionality in this description of revenge may derive from traditional conceptions of fair retribution in

Muslim jurisprudence, more important is its derivation of revenge from the enemy's own world. Retribution, in other words, does not enjoy any autonomy as an act here because it depends on the prior action of its foe—it cannot even legitimize itself by appealing to some external authority. Indeed its revenge belongs so wholly to the West that the jihad cannot take responsibility for it. And however self-serving this abandonment of responsibility might be, it confirms the jihad's place within rather than outside that world called Western. The interiority of the jihad to the West, and its consequent abandonment of responsibility for certain acts of terror, is not simply a rhetorical ploy but deadly in its earnestness. One of the Indian workers in Iraq taken hostage by the Islamic Secret Army, for instance, was pictured in a videotape released by the group dressed in what appeared to be the orange overalls worn by prisoners in Guantanamo Bay as well as in Abu Ghraib Prison.[8] And this sartorial distinction now appears to have become a standard element in Iraqi hostage-taking. It is a bizarre form of trading places that illustrates the intimacy between the jihad and its enemies.

Another form of reciprocity in the jihad's struggle with the West has to do with its desire for equal treatment. Thus Osama bin Laden in an interview with Al-Jazeera in October of 2001:

The killing of innocent civilians, as America and some intellectuals claim, is really very strange talk. Who said that our children and civilians are not innocent and that shedding their blood is justified? That it is lesser in degree? When we kill their innocents, the entire world from east to west screams at us, and America rallies its allies, agents, and the sons of its agents. Who said that our blood is not blood, but theirs is? Who made this pronouncement? Who has been getting killed in our countries for decades? More than 1 million children, more than 1 million children died in Iraq and others are still dying. Why do we not hear someone screaming or condemning, or even someone's words of consolation or condolence?

How come millions of Muslims are being killed? Where are the experts, the writers, the scholars and the freedom fighters, where are the ones who have an ounce of faith in them? They react only if we kill American civilians, and every day we are being killed, children are being killed in Palestine. We should review the books. Human nature makes people stand with the powerful without noticing it. When they talk about us, they know we won't respond to them. In the past, an Arab king once killed an ordinary Arab man. The people started wondering how come kings have the right to kill people just like that. Then the victim's brother went and killed the king in revenge. People were disappointed with the young man and asked him, "How could you kill a king for your brother?" The man said, "My brother is my king." We consider all our children in Palestine to be kings.[9]

This rhetoric moves beyond the call for reciprocity in revenge to question the moral basis of retribution itself. In effect Osama bin Laden seems to be declaring any form of justice that is not globally impartial to be injustice, so depriving American retribution of all moral foundation for the jihad's killings. However disingenuous or woolly-headed, Bin Laden's call for such universal justice puts Al-Qaeda squarely in the ranks of global movements like environmentalism, which also belong to a post-Cold War world that must be dealt with as a whole and not by dividing it into zones of friendship and enmity. Like the advocates of such movements, he even speculates in the quotation above about the ethical as opposed to merely political or economic reasons for a hierarchy that classifies human lives into more or less valuable commodities according to race, religion, nationality or class. This is a fairly standard complaint voiced by all manner of people, but it is left for Bin Laden to lift it from a merely moralistic statement to the plane of ethics. For it is apparently in order to dismantle this hierarchy that he approves of attacks against American civilians! This is certainly a novel way of creating relations of equality, but one that works in the most visceral of ways, abandoning the empty verbosity of moral anguish as it does so.

Killing, then, has become the instrument of achieving equality with the enemy, as if it is only in this manner that the latter's much-vaunted democracy can be imbibed. That great cliché which is the equality of death, however, also assumes another countenance in that same interview with Bin Laden:

Just as they're killing us, we have to kill them so that there will be a balance of terror. This is the first time the balance of terror has been close between the two parties, between Muslims and Americans, in the modern age. American politicians used to do whatever they wanted with us. The victim was forbidden to scream or to moan.[10]

Here the Cold War's doctrine of deterrence, resulting in a balance of power, has been translated into a balance of terror. And the consequence of such a balance is not only deterrence, as in the Cold War, but communication as well. For if in a world of imbalanced terror the victims, according to Bin Laden, could not even be heard, a world of balanced terror also means the possibility of communication. Much more than hatred and violence, in other words, the jihad's quest for an equivalence of terror precipitates a common language between the holy war and its enemies. As Osama bin Laden puts it in his "Letter to America":

America does not understand the language of manners and principles, so we are addressing it using the language it understands.[11]

Here is an almost identical statement by Ayman al-Zawahiri from *Knights Under the Banner of the Prophet*, which argues that the national interest by which all American action is justified has become both immoral and impossible in a global context which demands a wider ethical vision:

In addition, we must acknowledge that the west, led by the United States, which is under the influence of the Jews, does not know the language of ethics, morality, and legitimate rights.

They only know the language of interests backed by brute military force. Therefore, if we wish to have a dialogue with them and make them aware of our rights, we must talk to them in the language that they understand.[12]

The metaphors of communication so frequently used to describe violence in the jihad are neither meaningless nor accidental. Such communicative violence, rather, is supposed to force the American people to exercise their democratic rights for the good, as the following quotations from Osama bin Laden exemplify:

I ask the American people to force their government to give up anti-Muslim policies. The American people had risen against their government's war in Vietnam. They must do the same today. The American people should stop the massacre of Muslims by their government.[13]

We however, differentiate between the western government and the people of the West. If the people have elected those governments in the latest elections, it is because they have fallen prey to the Western media which portray things contrary to what they really are. And while the slogans raised by those regimes call for humanity, justice, and peace, the behaviour of their governments is completely the opposite. It is not enough for their people to show pain when they see our children being killed in Israeli raids launched by American planes, nor does this serve the purpose. What they ought to do is change their governments which attack our countries. [...] The Western regimes and the government of the United States of America bear the blame for what might happen. If their people do not wish to be harmed inside their very own countries, they should seek to elect governments that are truly representative of them and that can protect their interests.[14]

However genuine or insincere this rhetoric, it brings us face to face with holy war as an ethical intervention in America's democracy, urging its citizens to vote as a moral duty and make sure they are being properly represented by their government. Nothing better illustrates the internality of the jihad to America's new world order than its attempt to participate in the latter's electoral politics. Al-Jazeera's broadcast of a videotape in which Osama bin Laden addressed America just four days before the presidential polls, on October 29 2004, suddenly allowed America's most wanted man to participate in its democracy, something that prompted speculation by political parties and the media about Bin Laden's effect on the electoral process. And he, quite like a presidential candidate, took the opportunity to lecture Americans on their democratic obligations and offered them a way of achieving the national security they so vehemently desired:

Your security is not in the hands of [Democratic presidential candidate John] Kerry or Bush or al-Qaida. Your security is in your own hands and each state which does not harm our security will remain safe.[15]

Bin Laden's audacity in mentioning Kerry, Bush and Al-Qaeda in the same breath, only to dismiss them all as having no true responsibility for American security, is breathtaking, though it does acknowledge the fact that an American election can never be a purely national affair because of its global repercussions. In this sense Bin Laden's intervention in the US elections, addressing the nation as a statesman, as if he were himself a candidate, did no more than open up the electoral process globally. This was not the first time that the jihad had participated in American democracy, even though such participation had sometimes lacked earnestness and even been satirical, as in the following message released to the London-based Arabic newspaper *Al-Quds al-Arabi* by the Abu Hafs al-Masri Brigades, which claimed responsibility for the Madrid bombing of March 2004:

A word for the foolish Bush. We know that you live in the worst days of your life in fear of death squads which spoilt your world and we are very keen that you do not lose in the forthcoming elections as we know very well that any big attack can bring down your government and this is what we do not want. We cannot get anyone who is more foolish than you, who uses force instead of wisdom and diplomacy. Your stupidity and religious extremism is what we want as our people will not awaken from their deep sleep except when there is an enemy.[16]

Satire apart, this statement assumes a position so internal to American democracy as to reverse the roles assigned to Washington's opponents in the war on terror, with President Bush being described as a religious extremist who uses force instead of diplomacy. In his intervention in the 2004 American elections, Osama bin Laden used the same procedure of satirical reversal to describe the Bush administration and his intimate knowledge of its ways:

We had no difficulty in dealing with Bush and his administration because they resemble the regimes in our countries, half of which are ruled by the military and the other half by the sons of kings. [...] They have a lot of pride, arrogance, greed and thievery.

[Bush] adopted despotism and the crushing of freedoms from Arab rulers—called it the Patriot Act under the guise of combating terrorism.[17]

For a man on the run, such refined rhetoric about the American leader's parentage and his militarization of the presidency is extraordinary. As is the detailed knowledge it presupposes of political debate in the United States, including allegations of corruption in the administration's relations with Saudi Arabia or in the awarding of contracts for Iraq's re-construction. There is even a suggestion that Osama bin Laden might have been familiar with Michael Moore's polemical film *Fahrenheit 9/11*, given his description of President Bush's initial reaction upon being told of the attacks on the World Trade Center:

It never occurred to us that the commander-in-chief of the American forces [Bush] would leave 50,000 citizens in the two towers to face those horrors alone at a time when they most needed him because he thought listening to a child discussing her goat and its ramming was more important than the planes and their ramming of the skyscrapers.[18]

Here we even have an acknowledgement of the "horrors" endured by the victims of the World Trade Center bombings, which is as illustrative of the jihad's sense of familiarity with the West as are its deployment of satire and reversal. Indeed so intimately does this joking relationship tie Osama bin Laden to the West that he even seems to admire the freedoms represented by Sweden as a model welfare state when rejecting President Bush's allegation that Al-Qaeda hated freedom:

Let him tell us why we did not attack Sweden for example.[19]

Needless to say the Muslim world as a whole, militant or quiescent, is approached in the media and by US commentators from the opposite direction, generally by way of traditional ideas about its exoticism and impenetrability. It is contrasts such as these that prove the claim made by *The 9/11 Commission Report*, with which I began chapter one, that the members of Al-Qaeda were more globalized than were Americans. And this precisely because they were weaker than their enemies and much further removed from the latter's instrumental politics of prognostication and control. The jihad's intimacy with the West goes beyond the violent persuasiveness of old-fashioned terrorism, and is in fact only possible given its interiority to this West as a global entity. Such intimacy finally ends in an acknowledgement of the West's potential humanity and the desire for a perfectly ordinary community with it. So in his interview with Hamid Mir for the Pakistani newspaper *Dawn* in November of 2001, Osama bin Laden makes the following observations:

HM: Demonstrations are being held in many European countries against American attacks on Afghanistan. Thousands of the protesters were non-Muslims. What is your opinion about those non-Muslim protesters?

OSB: There are many innocent and good-hearted people in the West. American media instigates them against Muslims. However, some good-hearted people are protesting against American attacks because human nature abhors injustice. The Muslims were massacred under the UN patronage in Bosnia. I am aware that some officers of the State Department had resigned in protest. Many years ago the US ambassador in Egypt had resigned in protest against the policies of President Jimmy Carter. Nice and civilized are everywhere. The Jewish lobby has taken America and the West hostage.[20]

Having conceded the possible humanity and justice of the West, Bin Laden immediately invokes a stereotype about the so-called Jewish lobby, thus placing the whole matter within the global context of a war inside the community of monotheists. But it is important to point out that this war, however vast its range and whatever its excesses, is by no means thought of as apocalyptic. Indeed I have already mentioned several times that the jihad lacks any notion of apocalypse, which is something far more characteristic of Christian (especially Protestant) and Jewish radicalism, with its talk of the rapture and the end of days, all of which spills over into the apocalyptic imagination even of profane movements like environmentalism. By a marvellous irony, then, the holy war, martyrdom operations and all, is fundamentally about life, while the West it fights appears to be singularly concentrated on death, even on the annihilation of humanity as a whole. Thus the concern in Euro-American cultures with every form and manner of disaster, from global warming to weapons of mass destruction. The jihad, however, is ethical in a worldly and even prosaic way, so that the end envisioned by it has nothing supernatural, rapturous or even final about it, and seems indeed to be something of an anti-climax. Here, for example, is a very typical passage illustrating the jihad's rather ordinary idea of finality from Osama bin Laden's 1997 interview with CNN:

REPORTER: Mr Bin Laden, if the Islamic movement takes over Saudi Arabia, what would your attitude to the West be and will the price of oil be higher?

BIN LADEN: We are a nation and have a long history, with the grace of God, Praise and Glory be to Him. We are now in the 15th century of this great religion, the complete and comprehensive methodology, has clarified the dealing between an individual and another, the duties of the believer towards God, Praise and Glory be to Him, and the relationship between the Muslim country and other countries in time of peace and in time of war. If we look back at our history, we will find there were many types of dealings between the Muslim nation and the other nations in time of peace and in time of war, including treaties and matters to do with commerce. So it is not a new thing that we need to come up with. Rather, it already, by the grace of God, exists. As for oil, it is a commodity that will be subject to the price of the market according to supply and demand. We believe that the current prices are not realistic due to the Saudi regime playing the role of a US agent and the pressures exercised by the US on the Saudi regime to increase production and flooding the market that caused a sharp decrease in oil prices.[21]

Does the jihad's very belief in the continuity of life allow it to defy death? Whatever the sufferings they claim to endure, the extinction of Islam is not a possibility contemplated by Muslim militants, let alone that of the entire world in some grand apocalypse. More important is the fact that the annihilation of enemies, as opposed to their mere defeat, also remains something un-thought in the jihad. There are routine mentions of the destruction of the Jews, whose egregious anti-Semitism differs from similar statements familiar to Europeans and Americans because they are in no case tied to a con-spiracy theory for which the Jews aim at world domination. Instead these anti-Semitic stereotypes are fragmentary and rarely linked to the analytical framework of the jihad as enunciated by an Osama bin Laden or an Ayman al-Zawahiri. And this framework, unlike Nazi or white supremacist theories, can well do without the malignity of the Jews, who as we have seen play no central role in it. But maybe it is precisely because of their marginal status in the logic of the jihad that the Jews can be treated so harshly by it.

Whether Jews, Christians or even the entire West are defined as Islam's enemies, the logic of genocide forms no part of the jihad's operations against them, however violent these latter may be. While the jihad in Western eyes, therefore, is often linked to an apocalyptic imagination for which genocide serves as a perfect complement, the violence of the holy war in the eyes of its proponents is not imagined in the terms of utter annihilation. It is quite unlike Jewish or Christian radicalism in this respect, which are much occupied by intimations of the world's end. So the jihad is modern in a Kantian sense because it is founded upon humanity's freedom from external or supernatural authority. As we have seen it is far more preoccupied with the death of God than that of man. Thus Osama bin Laden envisions the end of the holy war in the most ordinary terms, as is evident in his advice to Americans:

We also call you to deal with us and interact with us on the basis of mutual interests and benefits, rather than the politics of subdual, theft and occupation, and not to continue your policy of supporting the Jews because this will result in more disasters for you.[22]

Might the sheer normality of holy war here result from its lack of an apocalyptic imagination and therefore from its dedication to the continuity rather than the annihilation of life?

Western exposure

Since no external enemy is possible in the global order represented by the West after the end of the Cold War, and since the West has itself become a metaphysical rather than a geographical entity, its internal enemies are also metaphysical in nature. So the jihad, like other global movements emerging in the wake of the Cold War, has a different relationship to territory than the national or even imperial movements of the past, for which all political and economic interests were tied to possession. These movements were founded upon the control of land, resources and people who were defined in changeless racial or sexual terms. The holy war is metaphysical because, like other global movements, it is based on abstract phenomena like culture and civilization. If race and sex, then, were like property part of a political or economic order based on impermeable boundaries where mixing or miscegenation occasioned the greatest anxiety, religious and other global movements are part of an order where everything is variable and nothing impermeable.[23]

The post-Cold War redundancy of borders and therefore of old-fashioned possession, territorial or otherwise, transformed ethics and metaphysics into viable categories for all manner of global movements. And it is probably this viability that has also given religion a new lease on life, because it represents the victory of the spiritual over the material and cannot be confined within the borders of bodies as were race or sex, let alone within those of states. This is why the jihad aims not simply at protecting or defending the Muslims it sees as being under attack, but at gaining a metaphysical victory that is best defined by the word conversion. Conversion here is not in the least a political category premised on the possession of bodies or territories but an ethical one whose power is purely evidentiary. In other words, the victory of Islam is to be marked not simply by the independence and security of Muslims in their own lands, but also and simultaneously by the fall of the West from its position of metaphysical dominance. Indeed the one event implies the other, which is why Osama bin Laden exults in the attacks of 9/11 not for their homicidal success but because they presaged the disintegration of the West itself as a metaphysical entity defined by qualities like freedom and human rights. This is also why the ethics of the jihad are evidentiary in character, since they are meant to demonstrate the hollowness of the West morally as much as in any other way.

The hollowness of the World Trade Center, whose imposing towers crumbled so easily in the face of Al-Qaeda's attack, represented the void at the heart of Western civilization itself, not least because the attacks of 9/11 were followed by a significant if partial breakdown of America's much-vaunted culture of democratic rights and civil liberties, including even its suspension of certain provisions of the Geneva Conventions. This fact was not lost upon any participant in the jihad, to whom it demonstrated that the West's moral superiority was not only hypocritical, because its boasted freedom was based upon the un-freedom of others, but hollow as well, because it could not preserve this freedom even for its own citizens. And it is this hollowness that the jihad bears witness to in its acts of martyrdom, whose role is therefore evidentiary in character. Thus Bin Laden in an interview of 1998 with Al-Jazeera:

Following the absence of jihad from our Umat for such a long time we acquired a generation of people seeking education who had not experienced the reality of jihad, and they have been influenced by the American culture and media invasion that stormed the Muslim countries. Without even participating in a military war we find this generation has already been psychologically beaten.

What is true is that God granted the chance of jihad in Afghanistan, Chechnya and Bosnia and we are assured that we can wage a jihad against the enemies of Islam, in particular against the greater external enemy—the Crusader-Jewish alliance. Those who carried out the jihad in

Afghanistan did more than was expected of them because with very meagre capacities they destroyed the largest military force (the Soviet army) and in doing so removed from our minds this notion of stronger nations.

We believe that America is weaker than Russia and from what we have heard from our brothers who waged jihad in Somalia, they found to their greatest surprise the weakness, frailness and cowardliness of the American soldier. When only eight of them were killed they packed up in the darkness of night and escaped without looking back.[24]

Holy war here is considered an ethical phenomenon whose role is to bear evidence as much as it is to defend Islam or defeat its enemies. So the wars in Afghanistan, Chechnya and Bosnia are said by Bin Laden to be not heinous crimes against Muslims but heaven-sent opportunities to reaffirm the jihad as an ethical enterprise, one that had risked being abandoned by a new generation of Muslims. And what the jihad bore evidence to was the hollowness of American power and that of the West in general. In this context the attacks of 9/11 assume their importance as signs of America's vulnerability that no amount of shock and awe by the US military can undo. I turn now to examine how the jihad identifies and exploits this hollowness, which is as much metaphysical as it is military in nature.

Jurassic Park

Since the United States and its allies attacked and occupied Afghanistan and Iraq after the attacks of 9/11, there has been much loose talk among commentators about the founding of an American empire. These wars are certainly significant events, and precipitated novel forms of control and resistance, including the US military's extensive use of mercenaries and other private contractors who might work outside the bounds of the law, as well as the abduction and beheading by jihad groups of foreign nationals. Yet the invasion and occupation of foreign lands by the American military is hardly a new phenomenon and has never led to the establishment of an empire of whatever sort. Indeed the actions of the United States in Afghanistan and Iraq pale into insignificance compared with its conquest and occupation of Germany and Japan at the end of the Second World War.

The difference between those occupations and these is the fact that the enemy, and indeed war itself, have ceased to be territorial in important ways. For with the end of the Cold War and the beginnings of a global order in forms such as universal agreements over trade and security matters, the control of geography appears to have been relegated to the internal politics of nation states. At most, geography assumes international importance in the form of natural resources or strategic waterways, but certainly not as an object of old-fashioned conquest. Even at the height of the Cold War, incidents like the Suez Crisis of 1956 demonstrated that it was the control of routes like the Suez Canal rather than countries like Egypt that had become crucial. So for global movements like Al-Qaeda, as much as for global powers like the United States, territory serves only as a temporary base for some greater project, not as an object of desire or control in its own right. In fact the need to conquer and occupy parts of the world marks the weakness and not the strength of an invading force. This, at least, is the analysis of those who support the jihad, as Ayman al-Zawahiri points out:

Several indications are prominent in the US policy towards Islam, notably its basic role in establishing and aiding Israel. Except for Israel, which is in fact a large US military base, the United States did not resort in the past to conspicuous and intensive military presence to run its affairs in the Middle East until the second Gulf War erupted. When that happened, the United States rushed to the region with its fleets, its land troops, and air power to manage its own affairs with its own hands under the shadow of its own guns.

With this conspicuous US military presence, several new facts emerged including, first of all, the transformation of the United States from a mover of events from behind a veil to a direct opponent in its battle against the Muslims. Formerly, in both the Arab-Israeli conflict and in managing the internal affairs of other countries, the US administration used to portray itself as an impartial party, or at least as an indirect opponent that merely—as the US alleges—furthers the values of democracy, liberty, and Western interests. Now, however, the role of US power has become clear in attacking Iraq, defending the oil sources, and managing security affairs in some Arab countries.[25]

Finally dropping the anti-Semitic cliché that would have Israel controlling the United States, Zawahiri here describes it as a mere agent of America's global dominance. More than this, he claims that the long-standing policy by which the United States controls Middle Eastern oil through Israel and the Arab states has at last collapsed. The American military presence in the region, therefore, is a sign of weakness rather than strength. The United States, in Zawahiri's interpretation, has no intention of forming some kind of impossible empire either here or in Central Asia, but has been forced by circumstances beyond its control to assume the mantle of an occupying power. And as we know, this is exactly what Al-Qaeda would like America to do—become an old-fashioned empire and thus risk destruction like its erstwhile rival the Soviet Union. The task of the jihad, in other words, is to push the United States back into its Cold War role, so that it becomes like one of the genetically re-created dinosaurs in the film *Jurassic Park*. The jihad's struggle would then be one between a major but outmoded territorial power and a minor but futuristic global one, a struggle, shall we say, between politics and ethics? This is how Zawahiri sees it:

This policy, no matter how long it persists, is a short-term policy that will necessarily provoke repeated eruptions. However, what other alternative do the United States and Israel have? Allowing the fundamentalist movement any degree of freedom will shake the pillars of the pro-US regimes. Hence, a decision has been made to resort to the (repression by force) policy in order to close off the volcanic crater in the hope that the imposition of a fait accompli will cause a psychological change among the region's populations and that new generations will grow up who will forget their religious creed, which has been excluded from power, and their rights, which have been usurped. Furthermore the policy of dictating a fait accompli by force seeks to create new conditions in Muslim lands that it will be very difficult for any Islamist movement seeking to assume power to change except by a monumental effort, particularly in the early days of such a movement's rule. This provides a future guarantee for Israel's security. Nevertheless, history gives the lie to all such plans, for the Crusaders stayed in Greater Syria for 200 years but they had to leave even though they were a model of a settler occupation just like Israel today. Likewise communism was consigned to history and pursued by curses after seventy years of oppression, obliteration of identity, and population transfer.[26]

Liberal or leftist critics of the Bush administration often see its War on Terror as a choice rather than a necessity, an option offered to it by the immensity of American power. In their vision of things this choice, whether directed by special interests or national ones, is the kind of luxury that the United States cannot afford. The critics of the War on Terror, then, tend to adopt a moralistic tone when urging the administration to hold its power in check, predicting dire consequences otherwise. Their criticism is driven entirely by concerns about America's need for responsibility and self-control. Ayman al-Zawahiri views the conflict differently: for him it is not a choice but a necessity, one that betrays the failure rather than the success of American policy in the Muslim world. The United States, he claims, has been forced into a redundant war which it cannot win, since its aims, too, are redundant. Thus he compares American efforts to win hearts and minds with Soviet efforts to obliterate anti-socialist identities. These old-fashioned procedures of the Cold War, Zawahiri seems to be suggesting, did not work then and are unlikely to now.

Perhaps the wars in Afghanistan and Iraq were part of a gamble to transform American power in the new post-Cold War global landscape. But this is not what is significant about them. If Zawahiri's analysis has any truth to it, this war has little to do with American malignity and everything to do with the fact that a politics based on national causes is being made increasingly irrelevant by an ethics founded on global effects. The jihad is a global movement in this sense, a perverse call to ethics in an arena where old-fashioned politics can no longer operate—because it can no longer control. So it is ironic but not accidental that the Islamic Secret Army, which in July 2004 kidnapped several Indians together with an Egyptian and three Kenyans in Iraq, should have accused the Indian government precisely of "deviating from [Mahatma] Gandhi's path of peace".[27]

For its own part the US administration seems to recognize this new situation when it calls the deployment of its military and security apparatuses the "War on Terror", thus departing from the language of traditional politics for which the enemy was some particular entity—a group, a country, an ideology and even a phenomenon such as terrorism. By its very abstraction, the "War on Terror" leaves behind all enemies of a traditional kind to contend with something more metaphysical than empirical. This is one reason why the enemy in this war can become such a moving target: Al-Qaeda, the Taliban, Baathist Iraq. The list goes on because terror is something that may inhabit each one of these targets temporarily without being exhausted in any of them, not even in Islam itself as such a target. The "War on Terror" is not a war against Muslims, but, whatever its moments of opportunism, very literally a war on terror as a global and therefore metaphysical condition. The US Secretary of Defense himself noted this in an article published in 2002:

Our challenge in this new century is a difficult one: to defend our nation against the unknown, the uncertain, the unseen and the unexpected. That may seem an impossible task. It is not. But to accomplish it, we must put aside comfortable ways of thinking and planning—take risks and try new things—so we can deter and defeat adversaries that have not yet emerged to challenge us.[28]

Who are these unknown, uncertain, unseen, unexpected and even, for the moment, non-existent adversaries? They are enemies who inhabit the global landscape of the post-Cold War era. To identify them with Muslims or Islam might be comforting because it allows the dangers of this new world to be localized and castigated in a single name, but it is also short-sighted and dangerous, since the jihad only inaugurates this new world of dangers by providing an example of what else may come to pass. Jacques Derrida, in his astute reflections on the event that was 9/11, notes that the unknown future it opened was what made this event radically new: "The ordeal of the event has as its tragic correlate not what is presently happening or what has happened in the past but the pre-cursory signs of what threatens to happen. It is the future that determines the unappropriability of the event, not the present or the past."[29] And it is precisely this future that Osama bin Laden invokes. In his interview with *Ummat*, discussed above in chapter one, he seems to be evading responsibility for the attacks of 9/11 by suggesting that other groups and other aims might have been involved. What his words actually tell us is that any group or any aim could participate in such attacks, especially in the future that Al-Qaeda so skilfully inaugurated on that eleventh of September.[30]

The end of Islam

Following Al-Qaeda's 1998 bombing of the US embassies in East Africa, the world's press descended upon Osama bin Laden in his Afghan lair and among their many questions asked him to explain the significance of the name Al-Qaeda. It was as if the media, along with experts, specialists and scholars of all kinds, were intent on discovering the truth of his movement only in what was most foreign about it. This esoteric quest, while it provided much gainful employment for specialists, was curiously archaic in its episte-mology. What could better resemble colonial scholarship than these attempts to place the jihad within some exotic genealogy of its own, one that was completely separated from the larger world of ethics or politics? Even those who saw Al-Qaeda's actions in straight-forwardly political terms were loath to abandon the mysteries of its language. And yet none of these nineteenth-century style investi-gations could possibly deal with the jihad as a global movement, since all they did was locate it within a genealogy of scriptural inter-pretations. Was it Salafi? Was it Wahhabi?

Osama bin Laden himself seemed puzzled by enquiries about the significance of terms like Al-Qaeda, dismissing them as irrelevant and suggesting that the name was chosen in the most perfunctory of ways. And while this attitude may have indicated his effort to identify Al-Qaeda with the larger Muslim community, Bin Laden's rejection of an esoteric epistemology also illuminates the jihad's properly global character. Leaving aside its name, Al-Qaeda's language and practice in general have little to do with a secret truth that can only be known by Muslims immersed in an arcane tra-dition, or by the various kinds of experts trained in it. The very language of the jihad, after all, is English, which is not only used among operatives of different nationalities, but is, for instance, the

main language from which Osama bin Laden's various pronouncements are translated for Muslims across the globe.[31] The sheer
range of sources from which those involved in the global jihad
derive their ideas and information is staggering and gives the lie to
any theory that would associate militancy with a strictly confined,
madrasa-style, education. Most militants, after all, have received
not a religious but a secular education, and we know that in addition
to following the international media rather closely, many also seem
to be voracious readers in more than one language.

Among the files found on a computer used by Al-Qaeda members in Kabul, for example, are references to Aristotle, Jesus and
Menachem Begin's 1951 book, *The Revolt*, about his days as a terrorist fighting the British in Palestine—this being quoted approvingly and at great length.[32] There are also documents in Arabic,
Persian, Malay, French and English.[33] Even the videotapes of hostages held in Iraq are multilingual, their Arabic signs and statements
being juxtaposed with the hostages' own pleas and entreaties in
various languages. This immediately pluralizes the audiences of
these tapes and in fact presupposes their translation, thus under-
mining the idea of an original language for the Jihad. There is a sense
in which the jihad's globalization is facilitated by the English language, with Arabic continuing to play its usual role over most of the
Muslim world, as a minor language made for rituals rather than
ideas. But there is more to it than this:

UMMAT: The entire propaganda about your struggle has so far been made
by the Western media. But no information is being received from your
sources about the network of Al-Qaidah and its jihadi successes. Would
you comment?

Usama bin Laden: In fact, the Western media is left with nothing else. It has
no other theme to survive for a long time. Then we have many other things

to do. The struggle for jihad and the successes are for the sake of Allah and not to annoy His bondsmen. Our silence is our real propaganda. Rejections, explanations, or corrigendum only waste your time and through them, the enemy wants you to engage in things which are not of use to you. These things are pulling you away from your cause. The Western media is unleashing such a baseless propaganda, which makes us surprise[d] but it reflects on what is in their hearts and gradually they themselves become captive[s] of this propaganda. They become afraid of it and begin to cause harm to themselves. Terror is the most dreaded weapon in [the] modern age and the Western media is mercilessly using it against its own people. It can add fear and helplessness in the psyche of the people of Europe and the United States. It means that what the enemies of the United States cannot do, its media is doing that. You can understand as to what will be the performance of the nation in war, which suffers from fear and helplessness.[34]

This interchange not only suggests that Al-Qaeda is propagandized by its negative portrayal in the Western media, but also that this portrayal ends up retaliating against the West in the form of terror. Whatever the truth or falsity of this argument, it illustrates my own contention that the jihad is globalized as a series of effects rather than of causes—the latter having in fact vanished into the former. It is because Osama bin Laden recognizes Al-Qaeda's inability to practice a politics of control in its relations with the West, that he is able to separate the jihad's local causes from its global effects. And this means that the spectacular actions of a network like Al-Qaeda, while they are indeed meant to achieve certain goals, have nevertheless departed the realm of intentionality by relinquishing control over their consequences. They have become, in other words, symbolic acts, as Jean Baudrillard would have it, or ethical ones as I maintain they are.[35] I also maintain that as ethical practices, the acts of the jihad bear a family resemblance to those of other global movements like environmentalism or the anti-globalization protests, with which they share many other things besides, including forms of history and individuality.

Were a network like Al-Qaeda political in the instrumental way I am defining this term, it could be understood as easily as it would be dealt with, whether by force, negotiation or both. Its violence, however, is not instrumental and has no defined end, which is why it becomes impossible to deal with in purely political terms. Al-Qaeda is not the Mahdi Army, just as it is not Hamas nor even Hezbollah. On the other hand it is in some respects like its allies, the Sipah-e Sahaba or Jaish-e Muhammad, both groups that have little if any concern with states and territories—frequently betraying Pakistan's own national security for the cause of global Sunnism. Whatever the case, Al-Qaeda's brand of Islam resembles other global movements closely enough to move it beyond instrumental politics of a traditional kind. Olivier Roy, for example, argues convincingly that the kinds of individuals, practices and religiosity common to Al-Qaeda do not differ significantly either from quietist forms of Islam, or indeed from globalized religions more generally. For him such forms of Islam are both the agents and victims of globalization.[36]

But if the jihad shares so many features with non-violent forms of Muslim devotion, as well as with other, equally pacific global movements, then its militancy is by no means a stable phenomenon. Does violence therefore become an accidental factor in such movements? I would argue that the jihad is violent precisely because it is inherently unstable—because it can in fact turn into its opposite. This is an assumption on my part, but one that is based on the jihad's own ethical practice, which links it to non-violent movements like environmentalism or the anti-globalization protests. In other words it is the very fragmentation of Muslim practice in the jihad, or what I am calling Islam's democratization, that prevents it from becoming entrenched as a form of politics, and that consequently makes the jihad such an unstable phenomenon. Might Al-Qaeda's violence be the result of this very instability of the political in the age of globalization—which is to say the transformation of politics into ethics?

In the long run, violence is probably Al-Qaeda's most superficial and short-lived effect, though it is certainly one of great importance for the moment. Far greater and almost incalculable in its effects is the jihad's democratization of Islam, accomplished by its fragmentation of traditional forms of religious authority and the dispersal of their elements into a potentially endless series of re-combinations—some represented by Al-Qaeda itself. These possibilities have presented themselves because the jihad has put an end to old-fashioned fundamentalism as a movement dedicated to the establishment of an ideological state, itself a Cold War form, and because it has transformed Islam into a global phenomenon by placing ethics above politics. In a global environment where political control is being made archaic, all action becomes ethical as it loses instrumentality, coming thus to operate in a purely speculative way.

What this means for the history of modern Islam is that Al-Qaeda has assumed the role that had been assigned to Muslim liberals or modernists, as they are often known, of whom so much continues to be expected to this day. The holy grail of Islamic liberalism has been pursued relentlessly for some two hundred years now, but with little success. Such a thing does exist, but only as an intellectual movement. While liberal intellectuals are often great scholars of Islam, they have had little effect in the Muslim world unless allied to military strong men like Reza Shah in Iran, Mustafa Kemal Pasha in Turkey, or Ayub Khan and Pervez Musharaf in Pakistan. My own teacher, the celebrated modernist Fazlur Rahman, willingly served as a functionary in the regime of Pakistan's Field Marshal Ayub Khan—perhaps because, as he often used to say, liberalism by itself was toothless. In doing this, Muslim liberals are only following a great intellectual tradition, one that began with Plato and Dionysius or Aristotle and Alexander, and was still running strong with Voltaire and Frederick the Great, to say nothing of more recent examples like Heidegger and Hitler. In the United States today, this collaborationist tradition for which freedom is dictated by power, happens to be represented by neo-conservative intellectuals who claim to be the heirs of Leo Strauss.

The political allegiances of Muslim liberals are of little consequence compared to their intellectual stagnation. Whatever the merits of their scholarship, these men tend to follow schemes of Islamic reform propounded over a century ago by modernists like Sayyid Ahmad Khan. These include attempts to reinterpret the Quran and restructure Islamic law according to European models. Such reforms are then to be propagated by the state in forms like education. Not only is there nothing new in the nostrums hawked by Muslim liberals, unmitigated failures as the recent history of Islam demonstrates, they are not particularly adventurous either. Indeed it seems that the more such intellectuals depart from traditional interpretations of Muslim practice, the more respect they accord these, perhaps because the history of Islam has become a part of their cultural identity, and so an aesthetic rather than religious object.

It is ironic that liberals should adopt the most conservative of attitudes towards the Islamic tradition—so much so that even their most basic formulations, like returning to the original sources of Islam, have been left for the fundamentalists to develop. These fundamentalists, on the other hand, for whom Islam is a site not of identity but citizenship, have always been far less respectful about the historical corpus of their religion, often altering or even abandoning portions of it to make it more modern. Their task after all is to translate Islam into the language of the ideological state. But it is the jihad that completely fragments this tradition, with Osama bin Laden and Ayman al-Zawahiri proving themselves to be greater revolutionaries by far than their liberal predecessors, whose heirs in the task of Islam's transformation they properly are.

NOTES

Chapter 1 *Effects without causes*

1. *The 9/11 Commission Report: Final Report of the National Commission on Terrorist Attacks Upon the United States* (New York: W.W. Norton, 2004), pp. 339–40.

2. Jean Genet, *Prisoner of Love*, trans. Barbara Bray (Hanover, NH: Wesleyan University Press, 1992), p. 95.

3. While I am aware of the long philosophical tradition in which the terms politics and ethics have been related, I use them here in an everyday sense: standing in for actions that are meant to be instrumental on the one hand and for those that are not on the other. Whether such distinctions are in reality possible is another matter. I shall return to the jihad's ethics below.

4. See, for example, "Terror Suspect", Bin Laden's interview with Rahimullah Yousafsai for ABC News, Dec. 22, 1998 (http://abcnews.go.com/sections/world/DailyNews/transcript_binladen1_981228.html).

5. See, Bin Laden's interview with CNN, March 1997 (http://www.news.findlaw.com/cnn/docs/binladen/binladenintvw-cnn.pdf).

6. See Olivier Roy, *Globalised Islam: The Search for a New Ummah* (London: Hurst, 2004).

7. "Usama bin Laden says the Al-Qaidah group had nothing to do with the 11 September attacks", *Ummat*, Karachi, Sept. 28, 2001 (http://www.robert-fisk.com/usama_interview_ummat.htm), p. 2.

8. Quoted in Yosri Fouda and Nick Fielding, *Masterminds of Terror* (New York: Arcade Publishing, 2003), pp. 117–18.

9. Ibid., p. 118.

10. For the disagreement, rancour and even corruption in Al-Qaeda's network, which reveals its members to be quite unlike the fanatically unified storm-troopers of popular imagination, see Alan Cullison, "Inside Al-Qaeda's hard drive", *The Atlantic Monthly*, Sept. 2004, pp. 55–70.

11. There is much discomfort among advocates of global movements about acknowledging their kinship with Al-Qaeda, whose notable similarities to

165

their own groups have to be repeatedly exorcised. So Michael Hardt and Antonio Negri, in their recent study of these global networks, frequently raise the spectre of Al-Qaeda only to lay it to rest by claiming that it is not a true network because it is centralized and has a vertical command structure. We shall see later that this is not quite true, but even if it were, the authors' unwillingness to discuss the many points that the jihad has in common with more presentable movements for social justice remains puzzling. Surely these similarities not only reinforce Hardt and Negri's argument on the emergence of the network as a new organizational form, but they also allow for a much more complex analysis of it. See Michael Hardt and Antonio Negri, *Multitude: War and Democracy in the Age of Empire* (New York: The Penguin Press, 2004).

12. "Transcript of Usama Bin Laden Video Tape", translated by George Michael and Kassem M. Wahba, Dec. 13, 2001, (http://www.defenselink.mil/news/Dec2001/d20011213ubl.pdf), p. 3. All parentheses mine.

13. See, for example, "Interview with Osama Bin Laden", a conversation between Bin Laden and some of his followers, May 1998 (http://www.pbs.org/wgbh/pages/frontline/shows/binladen/who/interview.html), p. 3.

14. For an analysis of the series of global effects that made this odd couple possible, see David Pedersen, "As Irrational as Bert and Bin Laden: The Production of Categories, Commodities, and Commensurability in the Era of Globalization", *Public Culture*, vol. 15, no. 2, Spring 2003, pp. 239–59.

15. "Piecing together Madrid bombers' past", BBC News, 2004/04/05, (http://news.bbc.co.uk/go/pr/fr/-/1/hi/world/europe/3600421.stm), p. 1.

16. Quoted in Yosri Fouda and Nick Fielding, *Masterminds of Terror*, p. 120.

17. See, for instance, Bin Laden's interview of Sept. 28, 2001 with the Pakistani newspaper *Ummat*, titled "Usama bin Laden says the Al-Qaidah group had nothing to do with the 11 September attacks" (http://www.robert-fisk.com/usama_interview_ummat.htm).

18. See, for instance, Alan Cullison, "Inside Al-Qaeda's hard drive", pp. 55–70.

19. Ibid., p. 62.

20. Ibid., p. 127.

21. For these details see *The 9/11 Commission Report: Final Report of the National Commission on Terrorist Attacks Upon the United States* (New York: W. W. Norton, 2004), esp. chs 5 and 7.

22. This is made clear in Marc Sageman's *Understanding Terror Networks* (Philadelphia: University of Pennsylvania Press, 2004), which examines the backgrounds of some 200 Al-Qaeda operatives.

23. Jessica Stern, *Terror in the Name of God* (New York: Harper Collins, 2003), p. 75.

24. Reinhard Schulze, *A Modern History of the Islamic World*, trans. Azizeh Azodi (New York University Press, 2002).

25. See, for instance, the Pentagon's "Investigation of the Abu Ghraib detention facility and 205th Military Intelligence Brigade", in Steven Strasser (ed.), *The Abu Ghraib Investigations* (New York: Public Affairs, 2004), p. 160.

26. For details of such incidents see the two official reports included in *The Abu Ghraib Investigations*.

27. Roxanne Euben, *Enemy in the Mirror: Islamic Fundamentalism and the Limits of Modern Rationalism* (Princeton University Press, 1999).

28. Seyyed Vali Reza Nasr, *Vanguard of the Islamic Revolution: the Jamaat-i Islami of Pakistan* (Berkeley: University of California Press, 1994), and *Mawdudi and the Making of Islamic Revivalism* (New York: Oxford University Press, 1996).

29. Olivier Roy, *The Failure of Political Islam*, trans. Carol Volk (Cambridge, MA: Harvard University Press, 1994).

30. "Extracts from Al-Jihad Leader Al-Zawahiri's New Book", *al-Sharq al-Awsat*, http://www.fas.org/irp/world/para/ayman_bk.html, p. 77.

31. Ibid., pp. 44–5.

32. Ibid., p. 80.

33. Olivier Roy describes extensively this new form of Muslim individualization in the fourth chapter of his *Globalised Islam*.

34. Quoted in Quintan Wictorowicz and John Kaltner, "Killing in the Name of Islam: Al-Qaeda's Justification for September 11", *Middle East Policy Council Journal*, vol. X, no. 2, Summer 2003, p. 2.

Chapter 2 *A Democratic History of Holy War*

1. The Middle East Media Research Institute, Jihad and Terrorism Studies Project, Special Dispatch Series, no. 650, Jan. 27, 2004 (http://www.memri.org/bin/articles.cgi?Page=subjects&Area=jihad&ID=sp65004), p. 2.

2. "Usama bin Laden says the Al-Qaidah group had nothing to do with the 11 September attacks", *Ummat*, Karachi, Sept. 28, 2001 (http://www.robert-fisk.com/usama_interview_ummat.htm), p. 3.

3. W. W. Hunter, *The Indian Musulmans: Are They Bound in Conscience to Rebel Against the Queen?* (New Delhi: Indological Book House, 1969), p. 136.

4. Ibid., p. 205.

5. Sayyid Ahmad Khan, *Review on Dr. Hunter's Indian Musalmans: Are They Bound in Conscience to Rebel Against the Queen?* (Lahore: Premier Book House, n.d.), pp. 5–6.

6. Ibid., p. 45.

7. For a very different view of Muslim history, see Richard Bulliet, *Islam: The View From the Edge* (New York: Columbia University Press, 1993).

8. See, for instance, Bin Laden's interview with ABC News producer Rahimullah Yousafsai on Dec. 22, 1998 (http://abcnews.go.com/sections/world/Daily-News/transcript_binladen1_981228.html), p. 3.

9. Roy, *Globalised Islam*, p. 246.

10. William Dalrymple, "Inside Islam's "terror schools"", *New Statesman and Society, March 28 2005 http://www.newstatesman.com/200503280010*

11. "Azzam.com correspondent Suraqah al-Andalusi, killed by cluster bomb in Battle for Tora Bora 14 December 2001 at 28 years" (http://www.zawaj.com/azzam/suraqah_al_andulusi.html#brother), p. 10.

12. Ibid., p. 5.

13. Jean Baudrillard, *The Gulf War Did Not Take Place*, trans. Paul Patton (Bloomington and Indianapolis: Indiana University Press, 1995), pp. 36–7.

14. Ayman al-Zawahiri, "Extracts from Al-Jihad Leader Al-Zawahiri's New Book", *Al-Sharq al-Awsat* (http://www.fas.org/irp/world/para/ayman_book.html), p. 61.

15. The breakdown of traditional forms of authority in the Muslim world has assumed the status of an academic cliché. For a classic account, see Dale Eickelman and James Piscatori, *Muslim Politics* (Princeton University Press, 1996).

16. Zawahiri, p. 46.

17. For the "Rushdie Affair" as an example of Islam's first global movement, see Devji, "Imitatio Muhammadi: Khomeini and the Mystery of Citizenship", *Cultural Dynamics*, vol. 13, no. 3 (2001), pp. 363–71.

18. For his comment on Iran, see John Miller's interview of Bin Laden in May, 1998 for ABC News (http://www.pbs.org/wgbh/pages/frontline/shows/binladen/who/interview.html), p. 9. For the vision of a pluralist Islam, see Bin Laden's interview with the magazine *Nida'ul Islam* published in its fifteenth issue of Oct.–Nov. 1996 (http://www.islam.org.au/articles/15/LADIN.HTM), p. 7.

19. *The 9/11 Commission Report*, pp. 240–1.

20. "Document: declaration of war against the Americans occupying the land of the two holy places (expel the infidels from the Arab Peninsula): a message from Usama bin Muhammad bin Laden to his Muslim brethren all over the world generally and in the Arab Peninsula specifically", reprinted in *The Idler*, vol. 3, no. 165, p. 9. (http://www.geocities.com/dcjarviks//Idler/vIIIn165.html).

21. Mariam Abou Zahab and Olivier Roy, *Islamist Networks: The Afghan-Pakistan Connection* (London: Hurst and Co, 2004), p. 65.

22. See the fifth chapter of Muhammad Qasim Zaman, *The Ulama in Contemporary Islam: Custodians of Change* (Princeton University Press, 2002).

23. For another account of sectarian violence in Pakistan, see S. V. R. Nasr, "Islam, the State and the Rise of Sectarian Militancy in Pakistan", in C. Jaffrelot (ed.), *Pakistan: Nationalism Without a Nation?* (London: Zed Books, 2002).

24. See, for instance, Cole, *Roots of North Indian Shiism in Iran and Iraq*.

25. Such a democratic narrative of enmity, one that is phrased in the language of equality and fraternity, is by no means unique to Sunni militancy. Hindu radicals deploy an identical narrative in their often violent relationship with Muslims across the border in India. If anything, this demonstrates that there is nothing particularly Islamic—or particularly Hindu—about the language of Sunni sectarianism in Pakistan and Hindu nationalism in India.

Chapter 3   *Monotheist Geographies*

1. Zawahiri, p. 9.

2. Ibid.

3. Ibid.

4. Ibid., p. 11.

5. Ibid., pp. 11–12.

6. Ibid., p. 12.

7. Ibid.

8. See Juan Cole, *Sacred Space and Holy War: The Politics, Culture and History of Shiite Islam* (London: I. B. Tauris, 2002), esp. ch. 5.

9. Hegel comments on the distinctly Christian nature of this geography in one of his early essays, "Is Judaea, then, the Teuton's Fatherland?" See G. W. F. Hegel, *Early Theological Writings*, trans. T. M. Knox (Cambridge University Press, 1971).

10. A point made by Edward Said in the last chapter of *Orientalism* (New York: Vintage Books, 1978).

11. Zawahiri, p. 77.

12. Ibid.

13. See Tayseer Alouni's Oct. 2001 interview with Osama bin Laden (http://www.cnn.com/2002/WORLD/asiapcf/south/02/05/binladen.transcript/index.html), pp. 4–5 (parenthesis mine).

14. See Giovanna Borradori, *Philosophy in a Time of Terror: Dialogues with Jurgen Habermas and Jacques Derrida* (University of Chicago Press, 2003), p. 106.

15. "Transcript of Bin Laden's October Interview" (http://www.cnn.com/2002/WORLD/asiapcf/south/02/05/binladen.transcript/index.html), p. 2.

16. Ibid., p. 7.

17. Ibid., p. 9 (second parenthesis is mine).

18. Ibid., p. 8.

19. Samuel P. Huntington, *The Clash of Civilizations and the Remaking of World Order* (London: Simon and Schuster, 2002).

20. "Jihad against Jews and Crusaders" (http://www.fas.org/irp/world/para/docs/980223-fatwa.htm), p. 2.

21. "Interview with Osama Bin Laden" (http://www.pbs.org/wgbh/pages/frontline/shows/binladen/who/interview.html), p. 4.

22. Ron Haviv and Ilana Ozernoy, *Afghanistan: the Road to Kabul* (New York: de Mo, 2002), pp. 126–7.

23. "Osama claims he has nukes: if US uses N-arms it will get same response" (http://www.dawn.com/2001/11/10/top1.htm), p. 2.

24. "Interview with Osama Bin Laden" (http://www.pbs.org/wgbh/pages/frontline/shows/binladen/who/interview.html), p. 3.

25. "Document: declaration of war against the Americans…" *The Idler*, vol. 3, no. 165, p. 21 (http://www.geocities.com/dcjarviks//Idler/vIIIn165.html).

26. "Full Text: bin Laden's 'Letter to America'", *The Observer*, Nov. 24, 2002 (http://observer.guardian.co.uk/print/0,3858,4552895-110490,00.html), p. 2.

Chapter 4 *Media and Martyrdom*

1. "Azzam.Com correspondent Suraqah Al-Andalusi…", p. 3.

2. Slavoj Zizek, *Welcome to the Desert of the Real* (London: Verso, 2002).

3. For my comments on the nature of mass media I have relied extensively on Niklas Luhmann, *The Reality of the Mass Media*, trans. Kathleen Cross (Stanford University Press, 2000).

4. Fouda and Fielding, *Masterminds of Terror*, pp. 27–8.

5. "Agencies, Pakistani hostages executed in Iraq", *The Indian Express*, Mumbai edn, Friday, July 30, 2004, p. 10.

6. UNI, "Asha Parekh willing to appeal to abductors", *The Hindu*, Kochi, Aug. 8, 2004, p. 8.

7. Fouda and Fielding, *Masterminds of Terror*, p. 98.

8. I owe these ideas to a conversation with Satya Pemmaraju.

9. Roxanne Euben, in a fine essay on martyrdom in the jihad, argues that it may help to anchor a new political project by lending it a kind of existential weight. While I do not explore this line of thought here, the sociability of martyrdom that I am describing might reinforce her argument. See Roxanne Euben, "Killing (For) Politics: *Jihad*, Martyrdom, and Political Action", *Political Theory*, vol. 30, no. 1, Feb. 2002, pp. 4–35.

10. "Reuters' evidence of foreign fighters in Iraq", *The Indian Express*, Mumbai, Wed., July 7, 2004, p. 9.

11. "9th issue of online magazine 'Voice of Jihad' from Saudi Arabia", The Middle-East Research Institute, Jihad and Terrorism Studies Project, Special Dispatch Series no. 650, Jan. 27, 2004 (http://www.memri.org/bin/articles.cgi?Page=archives&Area=sd&ID=SP65004), p. 3.

12. Wictorowicz and Kaltner, "Killing in the name of Islam", p. 8.

13. "God knows it did not cross our minds to attack the towers", *The Guardian*, Oct. 30, 2004. (http://www.guardian.co.uk/uselections2004/story/0,13918,1339845,00.html), pp. 1–2.

14. Quoted in Ghassan Hage, "'Comes a Time we are All Enthusiasm': Understanding Palestinian Suicide Bombers in Times of Exighophobia", *Public Culture*, 15 (1), 2003, pp. 84–5.

15. "Extracts from Al-Jihad Leader Al-Zawahiri's New Book", *Al-Sharq al-Awsat* (http://www.fas.org/irp/world/para/ayman_bk.html), pp. 71–2.

16. Ibid., p. 48.

17. Niklas Luhmann, *The Reality of the Mass Media*, trans. Kathleen Cross (Stanford University Press, 2000), pp. 2–3.

18. Ibid., p. 16.

19. Ibid., pp. 68–9.

20. Ibid., p. 69.

21. Ibid., p. 94.

22. "Transcript of Usama Bin Ladin Video Tape", trans. George Michael and Kassem M. Wahba, Dec. 13, 2001, (http://www.defenselink.mil/news/Dec2001/d20011213ubl.pdf), p. 5.

23. Ibid., p. 5.

24. Ibid., p. 6.

25. "Azzam.Com correspondent Suraqah Al-Andalusi", p. 14.

Chapter 5   *The Death of God*

1. Jason Burke, *Al-Qaeda: Casting a Shadow of Terror* (London, I. B. Tauris, 2003), pp. 166–7.

2. "Atta's Will Found." Oct. 4, ABC News (http://printerfriendly.abcnews.com/printerfriendly/Print?fetchFromGLUE=true&GLUEService=ABCNewsCom), p. 1.

3. Ibid.

4. See Burke, *Al-Qaeda*, p. 79.

5. Susan Schmidt, "All Qaeda men don't swear by Laden: Report", quoted from a *Los Angeles Times/World Press* report in *The Indian Express*, Mumbai, July 24, 2004, p. 11.

6. "Extracts from Al-Jihad Leader Al-Zawahiri's New Book" (http://www.fas.org/irp/world/para/ayman_bk.html), p. 14 (parenthesis mine).

7. Ibid., p. 24.

8. Ibid.

9. Ibid., p. 60.

10. "Atta's Will Found", ABC News, Oct. 4 (http://printerfriendly.abcnews.com/printerfriendly/Print?fetchFromGLUE=true&GLUEService=ABCNewsCom), p. 1.

11. See, for instance, Muhammad Iqbal, *The Reconstruction of Religious Thought in Islam* (Lahore: Sh. Muhammad Ashraf, 1962), pp. 125–6.

12. Ruhollah al-Musavi Khomeini, *Akhirin Payam* (Tehran: Sazman-e Hajj-o Awqaf-o Umur-e Khayriyyat, 1361), p. 22.

13. Wiktorowicz and Kaltner, "Killing in the Name of Islam".

14. "Last words of a terrorist", *The Observer*, 30 Sept. 2001 (http://observer.guardian.co.uk/print/0,3858,4267264-102275,00.html).

15. Ibid., pp. 3–4.

16. "Full text: bin Laden's 'letter to America,'" *The Observer*, 24 Nov. 2002 (http://observer.guardian.co.uk/print/0,3858,4552895-110490,00.html), pp. 4–5.

17. Ibid., p. 5.

18. Ibid.

19. Ibid.

20. Ibid.

21. Ibid., p. 6.

22. Ibid.

23. "Extracts from Al-Jihad Leader Al-Zawahiri's New Book", p. 46.

24. "Document: declaration of war against the Americans…" *The Idler*, vol. 3, no. 164, p. 25 (http://www.geocities.com/dcjarviks//Idler/vIIIn165.html).

25. Ibid.
26. For a more detailed description of the Rushdie Affair and the image of the Prophet, see Devji, "Imitatio Muhammadi: Khomeini and the Mystery of Citizenship", *Cultural Dynamics*, vol. 13, no. 3 (2001), pp. 363–71.

Chapter 6 *New World Order*

1. For a masterly discussion of politics and territoriality, and especially of the rise of a hemispherical politics, see Carl Schmitt, *The Nomos of the Earth*, trans. G. C. Ulmen (New York: Telos Press, 2003).
2. See the eleventh chapter of Etienne Balibar's *We, the People of Europe?*, trans. James Swenson (Princeton University Press, 2004).
3. Baudrillard, *The Gulf War Did Not Take Place*, pp. 23–4.
4. See Giovanna Borradori, *Philosophy in a Time of Terror: Dialogues with Jurgen Habermas and Jacques Derrida* (University of Chicago Press, 2003), p. 95.
5. For this phenomenon of "autoimmunity", see the interview with Derrida in Borradori, *Philosophy in a Time of Terror*.
6. "Transcript of Bin Laden's October interview", (http://www.cnn.com/2002/WORLD/asiapcf/south/02/05/binladen.transcript/index.html), p. 3.
7. "Full text: bin Laden's 'letter to America,'" *The Observer*, Nov. 24, 2002 (http://observer.guardian.co.uk/print/0,3858,4552895-110490,00.html), p. 3.
8. Pranab Dhal Samanta, "Hostage deadline today, Govt sends out fresh appeal", *The Indian Express*, Mumbai edition, July 30, 2004, p. 1.
9. "Transcript of Bin Laden's October interview", (http://www.cnn.com/2002/WORLD/asiapcf/south/02/05/binladen.transcript/index.html), p. 5.
10. Ibid., p. 4.
11. "Full text: bin Laden's 'letter to America,'" *The Observer*, Nov. 24, 2002 (http://observer.guardian.co.uk/print/0,3858,4552895-110490,00.html), p. 3.
12. "Extracts from Al-Jihad Leader Al-Zawahiri's New Book", *al-Sharq al-Awsat*, http://www.fas.org/irp/world/para/ayman_bk.html, p. 72.
13. Hamid Mir, "Osama claims he has nukes: If US uses N-arms it will get same response", *Dawn*, November 10, 2001 (http://www.dawn.com/2001/11/10/top1.htm), p. 2.
14. "Interview with Osama bin Laden (May 1998)" (http://www.pbs.org/wgbh/pages/frontline/shows/binladen/who/interview.html), p. 4.

15. "God knows it did not cross our minds to attack the towers", *The Guardian*, October 30, 2004, (http://www.guardian.co.uk/uselections2004/story/0,13918,1339845,00.html), p. 2.

16. BBC News, "Extract: Al-Qaeda warns of more attacks", 2004/03/18 (http://news.bbc.co.uk/go/pr/fr/-/1/hi/world/europe/3523804.stm), pp. 1–2.

17. "God knows it did not cross our minds to attack the towers", *The Guardian*, Oct. 30, 2004 (http://www.guardian.co.uk/uselections2004/story/0,13918,1339845,00.html), p. 2.

18. Ibid.

19. Ibid., p. 2.

20. Hamid Mir, "Osama claims he has nukes: If US uses N-arms it will get same response", *Dawn*, Nov. 10 2001 (http://www.dawn.com/2001/11/10/top1.htm), p. 3.

21. "CNN March 1997 interview with Osama bin Laden" (http://www.news.findlaw.com/cnn/docs/binladen/binladenintvw-cnn.pdf), p. 2.

22. "Full text: bin Laden's 'letter to America,'" *The Observer*, Nov. 24, 2002 (http://observer.guardian.co.uk/print/0,3858,4552895-110490,00.html), p. 6.

23. For a discussion on the link between racial and national ideas, and of the breakdown of race as a bounded, physiognomic category in a global milieu, see Paul Gilroy, *Against Race: Imagining Political Culture Beyond the Color Line* (Cambridge, MA: Harvard University Press, 2000). The classic work on the breakdown of sex as a natural category is Judith Butler, *Gender Trouble: Feminism and the Subversion of Identity* (New York: Routledge, 1990).

24. "Text of al-Jazeera interview with Osama bin Laden (filed: 07/10/2001)" (http://news.telegraph.co.uk/news/main.jhtml?xml=/news/2001/10/07/wbin07.xml&amp) pp. 6–7.

25. "Extracts from Al-Jihad Leader Al-Zawahiri's New Book" in *al-Sharq al-Awsat*, http://www.fas.org/irp/world/para/ayman_bk.html, p. 42.

26. Ibid., p. 44.

27. Pranab Dhal Samanta, "Hostage deadline today, Govt. sends out fresh appeal", *The Indian Express*, Mumbai edn, July 30, 2004, p. 1.

28. Donald H. Rumsfeld, "Transforming the military", *Foreign Affairs*, vol. 81, no. 3, May/June 2002, p. 22.

29. Quoted in Borradori, *Philosophy in a Time of Terror*, pp. 96–7.

30. "Usama bin Laden says the Al-Qaidah group had nothing to do with the 11 September attacks", *Ummat*, Karachi, Sept. 28, 2001 (http://www.robert-fisk.com/usama_interview_ummat.htm), p. 2.

31. Sageman, *Understanding Terror Networks*, p. 163.

32. Cullison, "Inside Al-Qaeda's hard drive", p. 61.

33. Ibid., p. 56.

34. "Usama bin Laden says the Al-Qaidah group had nothing to do with the 11 September attacks", p. 4.

35. See Jean Baudrillard, *The Spirit of Terrorism*, trans. Chris Turner (London: Verso, 2002).

36. Roy, *Globalised Islam: The Search for a New Ummah* (London: Hurst, 2004).

INDEX

Abdel Kader (Rif), 35

Abu Ghraib Prison, 26, 92, 140, *see also* Iraq, US-led war in

Afghanistan and Afghanis: 10, 13, 24, 35, 43, 46, 53, 107, 109; and Britain, 36–7; and the jihad, 1, 4, 11, 21, 23, 27, 41, 46, 56, 61–5, 74, 91–2, 96, 110, 116, 130–1, 151–2; training camps in, 17–19, 73, 86, 106; and USA, 1, 8, 37, 46, 57, 74, 91–2, 130–1, 146, 152–3, 156; and USSR, 21, 28, 36, 56, 57, 64, 152; *see also* mujahideen, Taliban

Ahmadis, 55, 58

Al-Andalusi, Suraqah, 46–7, 87–8, 110

Al-Jazeera, *see* media

Al-Jihad, 10, 49–50, *see also* Al-Zawahiri

Al-Qaeda and its jihad: attacks of, *see* Kenya: attacks on US embassy in, September 11, 2001 attacks, Spain: Madrid attacks (April 2004), Tanzania: attacks on US embassy in; and authority and law, xiii, xv, 33–4, 42, 48–9, 51–4, 59–60, 61, 65, 88, 112–18, 119–25, 132, 134, 140, 149, 160, 161–2; causes of, xiv, 4–7, 9, 11, 19, 20, 29, 32, 74–81, 87, 96–8, 110, 139–43, 160;

centre versus periphery, 61–5, 84, 131; and Christianity/Christians, *see* Muslims and the Muslim/Islamic world; effects of, viii–xv, 1–4, 9, 11–16, 20, 24, 26, 32, 50–4, 87, 95, 99, 105, 110, 112, 122, 125, 138–9, 154–7, 160, 161–2, 164; and ethics, 11–13, 34, 39, 41, 42, 45, 46, 97, 99–104, 105, 107–10, 118–20, 125–34, 139, 141–2, 147, 150–2, 154–6, 158, 160–2; and fundamentalism and fundamentalists, 4, 26–32, 34, 104, 112, 119, 120, 124, 131, 162; genealogy of, 20–6, 41–2, 87, 112, 158–64; geopolitical landscape of, 61–5, 125–31; and global economy/marketplace, 9–13, 19, 73–4, 78, 110; and the global order, 137–9, 139–49, 150, 153–7; global versus local, 4, 11, 27–32, 54, 61–5, 69–70, 74, 87, 131, 160; globalization of, viii–xv, 1–4, 8–9, 11–16, 20, 24–6, 28–32, 63–5, 125–6, 130–4, 137, 141, 146, 150, 159–61; ideology of, xiv–xv, 19, 25, 27, 29, 50, 62, 64, 69, 74–86, 99–101, 115, 139–49; intentions of, xiii, 2–5, 6–7, 9, 11–12, 14–15,

177

Indonesia and Indonesians: 23; and the
jihad, 13

Iqbal, Muhammad, 123–4

Iran and Iranians: 22, 65, 67, 136,
162; as an Islamic state and the
Islamic Revolution in, 21, 27, 51–2,
53, 55, 56–7, 124–5; and the jihad,
51, 130; *see also* Iraq, Khomeini

Iraq and Iraqis: 22, 67, 71, 79, 136;
and Iran, 51; and the jihad, 27, 69,
74, 81, 90, 95, 96, 140, 156, 159;
Karbala and Najaf, 66; US-led war
in, 12, 25–6, 74, 92, 136–7, 140,
145, 152–4, 156

Islam: and authority, *see* Al-Qaeda and
its jihad, jihad; and ethics, 31, 118–
19, 125–8, 132; and fundamentalism, *see* Al-Qaeda and its jihad,
jihad, Muslims and the Muslim/
Islamic world; globalization of, *see*
Muslims and the Muslim/Islamic
world; and jihad, *see* jihad; and the
jihad, *see* Al-Qaeda and its jihad;
and law, *see* authority; and martyrdom, 93–5, 103, 118–123, 125–8;
and messianism, 47–9; and migration (*hijrat*) and migrants, 45–6;
and modernity, *see* Muslims and the
Muslim/Islamic world; and politics, *see* Muslims and the Muslim/
Islamic world; practices and beliefs
of, 16, 18, 20, 23, 51, 66, 81–2,
85–6, 93, 102, 114, 115, 121–3,
126–8, 139–40, 161–2, 163; the
Prophet Muhammad, 22–3, 43, 45,
50, 52, 59, 77–8, 83, 110, 112,
115, 123, 124, 125, 133–4; Quran,
xii, 17, 31, 44, 59, 83, 102, 122,

134, 163; schools of, *see* Muslims
and the Muslim/Islamic world; *see
also* Al-Qaeda and its jihad, jihad,
martyrdom and martyrs, Muslims
and the Muslim/Islamic world,
Shia, Sufi, Sunni

Islamic Jihad, 52

Islamic Secret Army, 90, 140, 156

Ismaili, *see* Shia

Israel and Israelis: viii, 51, 54, 65, 68,
74, 79, 83, 86, 97, 100, 143, 153–
5; Jerusalem, 66, 67, 69–70, 79,
121; *see also* Judaism, Palestine

Jaish-e Muhammad, 53, 56, 161

Jamaah al-Islamiyyah: 52, 115; Al-
Rahman, Umar Abd, 49–51

Jamaat-e Islami: 24, 27, 31–2; Mawdudi, Sayyid Abul Ala, 23, 27, 44

Jerusalem, *see* Israel

jihad: and authority and law, 33–4;
defensive, xii, 33; and ethics, 34,
36–41, 42, 132, 151–2; and fundamentalism, 33–4, 51–6; greater,
xii, 33–4; historical movements,
33–6, 41, 52, 83–4; and Islam, xv,
33–4, 64, 152; lesser, xii, 33–4;
and martyrdom, 94–5; as a mythical cause, 2–3; offensive, xii, 33;
and Sufism, 35, *see also* Sufi; versus
terrorism, 5, *see also* terrorism; and
violence, 132, 149; Western interpretation of, xii–xiv, 36–41, 42,
45, 65, 76, 99–100, 105, 149; *see
also* Al-Qaeda and its jihad, Islam,
martyrdom and martyrs, Muslims
and the Muslim/Islamic world

jihad, the, *see* Al-Qaeda and its jihad

Jordan and Jordanians, 24, 67